STORIES TOLD BY THE MOTHER

Stories Told by the Mother

1

SRI AUROBINDO ASHRAM
PONDICHERRY

First edition 2001
Seventh impression 2016

Rs 70
ISBN 978-81-7058-645-6

Published by Sri Aurobindo Ashram Publication Department
Pondicherry 605 002
Web http://www.sabda.in

Printed at Sri Aurobindo Ashram Press, Pondicherry
PRINTED IN INDIA

Compiler's Note

These stories are not just stories; they are revelations of living truths conveyed to us by the Mother. Apart from a few, the stories have been culled from her "Questions and Answers", the English translation of her "Entretiens" in French.

These anecdotes were first published in French in 1994 under the title "La Mère Raconte". Now, at the beginning of a new millennium, we are happy to publish an English version of them. If they bring the reader closer to the Mother, their purpose will be well served.

With love and gratitude for all she has given us - and is still giving - we offer this work at her feet.

Table of Contents

Can a Child Be Conscious of Its Inner Truth?	1
The Most Important Thing	3
The Golden Pencil	5
Half a Mango	7
The Boastful Master	9
To Know What One Wants	11
Aspiration in the Physical	13
Untidy Room — Untidy Mind	15
The Dancing Disorder	17
Laziness and "Tamas"	19
The Painter and His Violin	20
Instinct: the Psychic of Animals	22
Kiki in Trance	24
Kiki Stung by a Scorpion	27
Aspiration	31
The Greedy Goat	32
True Modesty	33
Wiser than Man	35
The Scientist and the Cobra	38
True Courage	40
The Subtle Body	44
The Power of Imagination	47
Optimism à la Coué	49
One Grape Every Two Steps	53
Food for a Nightmare	55
Friendship with the Sun	57

Shooting Star	59
Child Prodigies	61
Flowers Are Extremely Receptive	65
Six Hundred Vegetables	67
Vegetables Speak	69
Think in the Stomach	71
Art and Yoga	74
The Art of Japan	76
The Woman Who Knew How to Walk	81
How Mother Works in Our Consciousness	83
Tiger Becomes... Tiny Little Cat!	85
Alexandra David-Neel and Mr. Tiger	88
Atmosphere and Accidents	91
Premonitions	95
Subtle Visions	98
Sudden Wonder	101
Reminiscences of Tlemcen	103
The Aura of Sri Aurobindo	111
All the Clocks Had Stopped	113
You Are too Perfect to Be Here	116
Play and Consciousness	118
March Past	120
Where Do the Gods Come From?	123
Yusuf and the Little Mouse	126

Mother at the age of seven

Can a Child Be Conscious of Its Inner Truth?

Can a child become conscious of this inner truth like an adult?

For a child this is very clear, for it is a perception without any complications of word or thought — there is that which puts him at ease and that which makes him uneasy (it is not necessarily joy or sorrow which come only when the thing is very intense). And all this is much clearer in the child than in an adult, for the latter has always a mind which works and clouds his perception of the truth....

This little true thing in the child is the divine Presence in the psychic — it is also there in plants and animals. In plants it is not conscious, in animals it begins to be conscious, and in children it is very conscious. I have known children who were much more conscious of their psychic being at the age of five than at fourteen, and at fourteen than at twenty-five; and above all, from the moment they go to school where they undergo that kind of intensive mental training which draws their attention to the intellectual part of their being, they lose almost always and almost completely this contact with their psychic being.

If only you were an experienced observer, if you could tell what goes on in a person, simply by looking into his eyes!... It is said the eyes are the mirror of the soul; that is a popular way of speaking but if the eyes do not express to you the psychic, it is because it is very far behind, veiled by many things. Look carefully, then, into the eyes of little children, and you will see a kind of light — some describe it as frank — but so true, so true, which looks at the world with wonder. Well, this sense of wonder, it is the wonder of the psychic which sees the truth but does not understand much about the world, for it is too far from it. Children have this but as they learn more, become more intelligent, more educated, this is effaced, and you see all sorts of things in their eyes: thoughts, desires, passions, wickedness — but this kind of little flame, so pure, is no longer there. And you may be sure it is the mind that has got in there, and the psychic has gone very far behind.

8 January 1951

The Most Important Thing

Whatever the way we follow, the subject we study, we always arrive at the same result. The most important thing for an individual is to unify himself around his divine centre; in that way he becomes a true individual, master of himself and his destiny. Otherwise, he is a plaything of forces that toss him about like a piece of cork on a river. He goes where he does not want to go, he is made to do things he does not want to do, and finally he loses himself in a hole without having any strength to recover. But if you are consciously organised, unified around the divine centre, ruled and directed by it, you are master of your destiny. That is worth the trouble of attempting... In any case, I find it preferable to be the master rather than the slave. It is quite an unpleasant sensation to feel yourself pulled by the strings and made to do things whether you want to or not — that is quite irrelevant — but to be compelled to act because something pulls you by the strings, something which you do not even see — that is exasperating. However, I do not know, but I found it very exasperating, even when I was a very little child. At five, it began to seem to me quite intolerable and I sought for a way so that it might be otherwise — without people getting a chance to scold me. For I knew nobody who could help me and I did not have the chance that you have, someone who can tell you: "This is what you have to do!" There was nobody to tell me that. I had to find it out all by myself. And I found it. I started at five. And you, you were five long ago....

Voilà.

1 July 1953

The Golden Pencil

There is only one thing that can truly save you, it is to have a contact, even the slightest, with your psychic being — to have felt the *solidity* of that contact. Then you place whatever comes to you from this person or that circumstance in front of that and see whether it is all right or not. Even if you are satisfied — in every way — even if you say to yourself: "At last I have found the friend I wanted to have. I am in the best circumstances of my life, etc.", then put that before this little contact with your psychic being, you will see whether it keeps its bright colour or suddenly there comes a little uneasiness, not much, nothing making a great noise, but just a little uneasiness. You are no longer so sure that it was as you thought! Then you *know*: yes, it is that small voice which one must always listen to. It is that which is the truth and the other can't trouble you any longer.

If you come to the spiritual life with a sincere aspiration, sometimes an avalanche of unpleasant things falls upon you; you quarrel with your best friends, your family kicks you out of the house, you lose what you thought you had gained... I knew someone who had come to India with a great aspiration and after a very long effort towards knowledge and even towards Yoga. That was long long ago. At that time, people used to put on watch-chains and trinkets. This gentleman had a golden pencil which his grandmother had given him, to which he was attached as the most precious thing in the world. It was fixed to his chain. When he landed at one of these ports — at Pondicherry or perhaps elsewhere in India or at Colombo, I believe it was at Colombo — they used to get into small boats and the boats took you ashore. And so this gentleman had to jump from the gangway of the ship into the boat. He missed his step, somehow got back his balance, but he made a sudden movement and the little gold pencil dropped into the sea and went straight down into the depths. He was at first very much aggrieved, but he told himself: "Why, that is the effect of India: I am freed from my attachments...." It is for very sincere people that the thing takes such a form. Fundamentally, the avalanche of troubles is always for sincere people. Those who are not sincere receive things with the most beautiful bright colours just to deceive them, and then in the end to enable them to find out that they are mistaken! But when someone has big troubles, it proves that he has reached a certain degree of sincerity.

15 July 1953

Half a Mango

Mother, on January 6 you said, "Give all you are, all you have, nothing more is asked of you but also nothing less."

Yes.

What is meant by "all you have" and "all you are"?

I am going to tell you in what circumstances I wrote this; that will make you understand:

Someone wrote to me saying that he was very unhappy, for he longed to have wonderful capacities to put at the disposal of the Divine, for the Realisation, for the Work; and that he also longed to have immense riches to be able to give them, to put them at the feet of the Divine for the Work. So I replied to him that he need not be unhappy, that each one is asked to give what he has, that is, all his possessions whatever they may be, and what he is, that is, all his potentialities — which corresponds to the consecration of one's life and the giving of all one's possessions — and that nothing more than this is asked. What you are, give that; what you have, give that, and your gift will be perfect; from the spiritual point of view it will be perfect. This does not depend upon the amount of wealth you have or the number of capacities in your nature; it depends upon the perfection of your gift, that is to say, on the totality of your gift. I remember having read, in a book of Indian legends, a story like this. There was a very poor, very old woman who had nothing, who was quite destitute, who lived in a miserable little hut, and who had been given a fruit. It was a mango. She had eaten half of it and kept the other half for the next day, because it was something so marvellous that she did not often happen to get it — a mango. And then, when night fell, someone knocked at the rickety door and asked for hospitality. And this someone came in and told her he wanted shelter and was hungry. So she said to him, "Well, I have no fire to warm you, I have no blanket to cover you, and I have half a mango left, that is all I have, if you want it; I have eaten half of it." And it turned out that this someone was Shiva, and that she was filled with an inner glory, for she had made a perfect gift of herself and all she had.

I read that, I found it magnificent. Well, yes, this describes it vividly. It's exactly that....

And the beauty of the story I told you — moreover, there are many others like it here — is just this, that when the old woman gave, she didn't know that it was Shiva. She gave to the passing beggar, for the joy of doing good, of giving, not because he was a god and she hoped to have salvation or some knowledge in exchange.

11 January 1956

The Boastful Master

Ambition has been the undoing of many Yogis. That canker can hide long. Many people start on the Path without any sense of it. But when they get powers, their ambition rises up, all the more violently because it had not been thrown out in the beginning.

A story is told of a Yogi who had attained wonderful powers. He was invited by his disciples to a great dinner. It was served on a big low table. The disciples asked their Master to show his power in some way. He knew he should not, but the seed of ambition was there in him and he thought, "After all, it is a very innocent thing and it may prove to them that such things are possible and teach them the greatness of God." So he said, "Take away the table, but only the table, let the table-cloth remain as it is with all the dishes upon it." The disciples cried out, "Oh, that cannot be done, everything will fall down!" But he insisted and they removed the table from under the cloth. Lo, the miracle! The cloth and all that was upon it remained there just as though the table was underneath. The disciples wondered. But all of a sudden the Master jumped up and rushed out screaming and crying, "Nevermore shall I have a disciple, nevermore! I am accursed! I have betrayed my God." His heart was on fire; he had used the divine powers for selfish ends.

It is always wrong to display powers. This does

not mean that there is no use for them. But they have to be used in the same way as they came. They come by union with the Divine. They must be used by the will of the Divine and not for display. If you come across someone who is blind and you have the power to make him see — if it is the Divine Will that the man shall see, you have only to say, "Let him see" and he will see. But if you wish to make him see simply because you want to cure him, then you use the power to satisfy your personal ambition. Most often, in such cases, you not only lose your power but you create a great disturbance in the man. Yet in appearance the two ways are the same; but in one case you act because of the Divine Will and in the other for some personal motive.

14 April 1929

To Know What One Wants

You must be absolutely free. If you want to have the true yogic attitude, you must be able to accept everything that comes from the Divine and let it go easily and without regret. The attitude of the ascetic who says, "I want nothing" and the attitude of the man of the world who says, "I want this thing" are the same. The one may be as much attached to his renunciation as the other to his possession....

You can easily know when a thing comes from the Divine. You feel free, you are at ease, you are in peace. But when something presents itself to you and you jump at it and cry out, "Oh, at last I have it", then you can know for certain that it does not come from the Divine. Equanimity is the essential condition of union and communion with the Divine.

Does not the Divine sometimes give you what you desire?

Certainly. There was a young man who wanted to do Yoga. But he had a mean and cruel father who troubled him very much and tried to prevent him from doing it. He wished ardently to be free from the father's interference. Soon the father fell ill and very seriously; he was about to die. Whereupon the other side of the boy's nature rose up and he loudly bewailed the misfortune and cried. "Oh, my poor father is so ill! It is such a sad thing. Alas, what shall I do?" The father got well. The young man rejoiced and turned once more to Yoga. And the father also began again to oppose and torment him even more violently. The son tore his hair in despair and cried, "Now my father stands in my way more than ever."

The whole thing is to know exactly what one wants.

14 April 1929

The house on rue du Val de Grâce in Paris where Mother wrote her early "Prayers and Meditations"

Mother in Paris in 1897

Aspiration in the Physical

When I speak of aspiration in the physical I mean that the very consciousness in you which hankers after material comfort and well-being should of itself, without being compelled by the higher parts of your nature, ask exclusively for the Divine's Love. Usually you have to show it the Light by means of your higher parts; surely this has to be done persistently, otherwise the physical would never learn and it would take Nature's common round of ages before it learns by itself. Indeed the round of Nature is intended to show it all possible sorts of satisfactions and by exhausting them convince it that none of them can really satisfy it and that what it is really seeking is a divine satisfaction. In Yoga we hasten this slow process of Nature and insist on the physical consciousness seeing the truth and learning to recognise and want it. But how to show it the truth? Well, just as you bring a light into a dark room. Illumine the darkness of your physical consciousness with the intuition and aspiration of your more refined parts and keep on doing so till it realises how futile and unsatisfactory is its hunger for the low ordinary things, and turns spontaneously towards the truth. When it does turn, your whole life will be changed — the experience is unmistakable.

When, as a child, I used to complain to my mother about food or any such small matter she would always tell me to go and do my work or pursue my studies instead of bothering about trifles. She would ask me if I had the complacent idea that I was born for comfort. "You are born to realise the highest Ideal," she would say and send me packing. She was quite right, though of course her notion of the highest Ideal was rather poor by our standards. We are all born for the highest Ideal: therefore, whenever in our Ashram some petty request for more comfort and material happiness is refused, it is for your own good and to make you fulfil what you are here for. The refusal is actually a favour inasmuch as you are thereby considered worthy to stand before the highest Ideal and be shaped according to it.

1930-31

Untidy Room — Untidy Mind

People who don't know how to deal with things carefully, don't deserve to have them. Sri Aurobindo has often written on this subject in his letters. He has said that if you don't know how to take care of material things, you have no right to have them. Indeed this shows a kind of selfishness and confusion in the human being, and it is not a good sign. And then later when they grow up, some of them cannot keep a cupboard in order or a drawer in order. They may be in a room which looks very tidy and very neat outwardly, and then you open a drawer or a cupboard, it is like a battle-field! Everything is pell-mell. You find everything in a jumble; nothing is arranged. These are people with a poor little head in which ideas lie in the same state as their material objects. They have not organised their ideas. They haven't put them in order. They live in a cerebral confusion. And that is a sure sign, I have never met an exception to this rule: people who don't know how to keep their things in order — their ideas are in disorder in their heads, always. They exist together, the most contradictory ideas are put together, and not through a higher synthesis, don't you believe it: simply because of a disorder and an incapacity to organise their ideas. You don't need to speak even for ten minutes with people if you can manage to enter their room and open the drawers of their tables and look into their cupboard. You know in what state they are, don't you?

On the other hand, there was someone (I shall tell you who afterwards) who had in his room hundreds of books, countless sheets of paper, notebooks and all sorts of things, and so you entered the room and saw books and papers everywhere — a whole pile, it was quite full. But if you made the mistake to shift a single little bit of paper from its place, he knew it immediately and asked you, "Who has touched my things?" When you come in, you see so many things that you feel quite lost. And yet each thing had its place. And it was so consciously done, I tell you, that if one paper was displaced — for instance, a paper with notes on it or a letter or something else which was taken away from one place and placed in another with the idea of putting things in order — he used to say, "You have touched my things; you have displaced them, you have put my things in disorder." That of course was Sri Aurobindo! That means you must not confuse order with poverty. Naturally if you have about a dozen books and a very limited number of things, it is easier to keep them in order, but what one must succeed in doing is to put into order — and a logical, conscious, intelligent order — a countless number of things. It requires a capacity of organisation.

3 February 1954

The Dancing Disorder

Thought-control! Who can control his thoughts? Only those who have trained themselves to it, who have tried hard since their childhood.

There is the whole range, you see, from total lack of control, which for most people comes to this: it is their thoughts which rule them and not they their thoughts. The vast majority of people are troubled by thoughts they cannot get rid of, which literally possess them, and they don't have the power to close the door of their active consciousness to these thoughts. Their thoughts govern them, rule them. You hear people saying every day, "Oh! that thought, all the time it comes back to me, again and again, and I can't get rid of it!" So they are assailed by all kinds of things, from anxiety to ill-will and fear. Thoughts which express dread are extremely troublesome; you try to send them away, they return like a rubber band and fall back on you. Who has control? It requires years of labour and such a long practice. And so, to come to something which is not complete control but anyway already represents a stage: to have the ability to do this in your head (*Mother moves her hand across her brow*), to annul all the movements, to stop the vibrations. And the mental surface becomes smooth. Everything stops, as when you open a book at a blank page — but almost materially, you understand... blank!

Try a little when you are at home, you will see, it is very interesting.

And so, one follows the place in one's head where the little point is dancing. I have seen — I have seen Sri Aurobindo doing this in somebody's head, somebody who used to complain of being troubled by thoughts. It was as if his hand reached out and took hold of the little black dancing point and then did this (*gesture with the finger-tips*), as when one picks up an insect, and he threw it far away. And that was all. All still, quiet, luminous... It was clearly visible like this, you know, he took it out without saying anything — and it was over.

And things are very closely interdependent: I also saw the case when someone came to him with an acute pain somewhere: "Oh! it hurts here, oh! it hurts, oh!..." He said nothing, he remained calm, he looked at the person, and I saw, I saw something like a subtle physical hand which came and took hold of the little point dancing about in disorder and confusion, and he took it like this (*same gesture*) and there, everything had gone.

"Oh! oh! look, my pain has gone."

Voilà.

8 January 1958

Laziness and "Tamas"

Of course, laziness is a kind of *tamas,* but in laziness there is an ill-will, a refusal to make an effort — while *tamas* is inertia: one wants to do something, but one can't.

I remember, a long time ago, having been among some young people, and they remarked that when I decided to get up I used to get up with a jump, without any difficulty. They asked me, "How do you do it? We, when we want to get up, have to make an effort of will to be able to do it." They were so surprised! and *I* was surprised by the opposite. I used to tell myself, "How does it happen? When one has decided to get up, one gets up." No, the body was there, like that, and it was necessary to put a will into it, to push this body for it to get up and act. It is like that, this is *tamas. Tamas* is a purely material thing; it is very rare to have a vital or mental *tamas* (it may occur but through contagion), I believe it is more a *tamas* of the nerves or the brain than vital or mental *tamas.* But laziness is everywhere, in the physical, the vital, the mind. Generally lazy people are not always lazy, not in all things. If you propose something that pleases them, amuses them, they are quite ready to make an effort. There is much ill-will in laziness.

28 April 1951

The Painter and His Violin

This is something I have heard from my very childhood, and I believe our great grand-parents heard the same thing, and from all time it has been preached that if you want to succeed in something you must do only that. And as for me, I was scolded all the time because I did many different things! And I was always told I would never be good at anything. I studied, I did painting, I did music, and besides was busy with other things still. And I was told my music wouldn't be up to much, my painting wouldn't be worthwhile, and my studies would be quite incomplete. Probably it is quite true, but still I have found that this had its advantages — those very advantages I am speaking about, of widening, making supple one's mind and understanding....

Spontaneously, people who wish to keep their balance rest from one activity and take up another. Examples are always cited of great performers or great artists or great scientists who have a kind of hobby, a diversion. You have perhaps heard of Ingres's violin. Ingres was a painter; he did not lack talent and when he had some free time he started playing the violin, and his violin interested him much more than his painting. It seems he did not play the violin very well but it interested him more. And his painting he did very well and it interested him less. But I believe that was quite simply because he needed balance. Concentration on a single thing in order to attain one's aim is very necessary for the human mind in its normal functioning, but one can arrive at a different working that's more complete, more subtle. Naturally, physically one is bound to be limited, for in physical life one depends a great deal on time and space, and also it is difficult to realise great things without special concentration. But if one wants to lead a higher and deeper life, I believe one can acquire perhaps much greater capacities by other means than those of restriction and limitation. There is a considerable advantage in getting rid of one's limits, if not from the point of view of realisation in action, at least from that of spiritual realisation.

10 February 1954

Instinct: the Psychic of Animals

In animals there is sometimes a very intense psychic truth. Naturally, I believe that the psychic being is a little more formed, a little more conscious in a child than in an animal. But I have experimented with animals, just to know; well, I assure you that in human beings I have rarely come across some of the virtues which I have seen in animals, very simple, unpretentious virtues. As in cats, for example: I have studied cats a lot; if one knows them well they are marvellous creatures. I have known mother-cats which have sacrified themselves entirely for their babies — people speak of maternal love with such admiration, as though it were purely a human privilege, but I have seen this love manifested by mother-cats to a degree far surpassing ordinary humanity. I have seen a mother-cat which would never touch her food until her babies had taken all they needed. I have seen another cat which stayed eight days beside her kittens, without satisfying any of her needs because she was afraid to leave them alone; and a cat which repeated more than fifty times the same movement to teach her young one how to jump from a wall on to a window, and I may add, with a care, an intelligence, a skill which many uneducated women do not have. And why is it thus ? — because there was no mental intervention. It was altogether spontaneous instinct. But what is instinct? — it is the presence of the Divine in the genius of the species, and that, that is the psychic of animals; a collective, not an individual psychic.

I have seen in animals all the reactions, emotional, affective, sentimental, all the feelings of which men are so proud. The only difference is that animals cannot speak of them and write about them, so we consider them inferior beings because they cannot flood us with books on what they have felt.

8 January 1951

Kiki in Trance

These extraordinary animals, do they come back in a human body after death?

Ah!

There was a cat... what its name was I don't know; and I had many cats, you know, so I don't remember now, there was one called Kiki, it was the first son of this cat, and then there was another, its second son (that is to say, born another time) which was called Brownie.

This one was admirable and it died of the cat disease — as there is a disease of the dogs, there is a disease of the kittens — I don't know how it caught the thing, but it was wonderful during its illness and I was taking care of it as of a child. And it always expressed a kind of aspiration. There was a time before it fell ill... we used to have in those days meditation in a room of the Library House, in the room there — Sri Aurobindo's own room — and we used to sit on the floor. And there was an armchair in a corner, and when we gathered for the meditation this cat came every time and settled in the armchair and literally it entered into a trance, it had movements of trance; it did not sleep, it was not asleep, it was truly in a trance; it gave signs of that and had astonishing movements, as when animals dream; and it didn't want to come out from it, it refused to come out, it remained in it for hours. But it never came in until we were beginning

Drawing by Mother

the meditation. It settled there and remained there throughout the meditation. We indeed had finished but it remained, and it was only when I went to take it, called it in a particular way, brought it back into its body, that it consented to go away; otherwise no matter who came and called it, it did not move. Well, this cat always had a great aspiration, a kind of aspiration to become a human being, and in fact, when it left its body it entered a human body. Only it was a very tiny part of the consciousness, you see, of the human being... this one was a cat which leaped over many births, so to say, many psychic stages to enter into contact with a human body. It was a simple enough human body, but still, all the same... There is a difference in the development of a cat and of a human being...

It happens... I think these are exceptional cases, but still it happens.

In these cases is the psychic conscious?

The aspiration is conscious, yes, conscious. The aspiration was very conscious in it, very conscious. It is not a formed psychic as when the psychic becomes a completely independent being, it is not that; but it is an aspiration, it is an ardent aspiration for progress — as we, you know, we have the aspiration to become supramental beings instead of remaining human beings, well, it was something absolutely similar: it was a cat doing yoga — exactly — to become a man.

It was perhaps because its mother had in it a movement, a formation, an emanation of consciousness which had belonged to a human being; it is probably that which had left a kind of nostalgia for the human life which gave it this intensity of aspiration. But truly it did yoga for that.

23 March 1955

Kiki Stung by a Scorpion

Animals have much more perfect senses than those of men. I challenge you to track a man as a dog does, for instance!

This means that in the curve or rather the spiral of evolution, animals (and more so those we call "higher" animals, because they resemble us more closely) are governed by the spirit of the species which is a highly conscious consciousness. Bees, ants, obey this spirit of the species which is of quite a special quality. And what is called "instinct" in animals is simply obedience to the spirit of the species which always knows what ought and ought not to be done. There are so many examples, you know. You put a cow in a meadow; it roams around, sniffs, and suddenly puts out its tongue and snatches a blade of grass. Then it wanders about again, sniffs and gets another tuft of grass, and so it goes on. Has anyone ever known a cow under these conditions eating poisonous grass? But shut this poor animal up in a cow-shed, gather and put some grass before it, and the poor creature which has lost its instinct because it now obeys man (excuse me), eats the poisonous grass along with the rest of it. We have already had three such cases here, three cows which died of having eaten poisonous grass. And these unfortunate animals, like all animals, have a kind of respect (which I could call unjustifiable) for the superiority of man — if he puts poisonous grass before the cow and tells it to eat, it eats it!

But left to itself, that is, without anything interfering between it and the spirit of the species, it would never do so. All animals which live close to man lose their instinct because they have a kind of admiration full of devotion for this being who can give them shelter and food without the least difficulty — and a little fear too, for they know that if they don't do what man wants they will be beaten!

It is quite strange, they lose their ability. Dogs, for instance the sheep-dog which lives far away from men with the flocks and has a very independent nature (it comes home from time to time and knows its master well, but often does not see him), if it is bitten by a snake, it will remain in a corner, lick itself and do all that is necessary till it gets cured. The same dog, if it stays with you and is bitten by a snake, dies quietly like man.

I had a very sweet little cat, absolutely civilised, a marvellous cat. It was born in the house and it had the habit all cats have, that is to say, if something moved, it played with that. Just then there was in the house a huge scorpion; as was its habit, the cat started playing with the scorpion. And the scorpion stung it. But it was an exceptional cat; it came to me, it was almost dying, but it showed me its paw where it was bitten — it was already swollen and in a terrible state. I took my little cat — it was really sweet — and put it on a table and called Sri Aurobindo. I told him, "Kiki has been stung by a scorpion, it must be cured." The cat stretched its neck and looked at Sri Aurobindo, its eyes already a little glassy. Sri Aurobindo sat before it and looked at it also. Then we saw this little cat gradually beginning to recover, to come round, and an hour later it jumped to its feet and went away completely healed.... In those days, I had the habit of holding a meditation in the room where Sri Aurobindo slept (the room A. uses now) and it was regularly the same people who came; everything was arranged. But there was an armchair in which this very cat always settled beforehand — it did not wait for anyone to get into the chair, it got in first itself! And regularly it went into a trance! It was not sleeping, it was not in the pose cats take when sleeping: it was in a trance, it used to start up, it certainly had visions. And it let out little sounds. It was in a profound trance. It remained thus for hours together. And when it came out from that state, it refused to eat. It was awakened and given food, but it refused: it went back to its chair and fell again into a trance! This was becoming very dangerous for a little cat... But this was not an ordinary cat.

To finish my story, if you leave an animal in its normal state, far from man, it obeys the spirit of the species, it has a very sure instinct and it will never commit any stupidities. But if you take it and keep it with you, it loses its instinct, and it is then you who must look after it, for it no longer knows what should or should not be done. I was interested in cats to make an experiment, a sort of inverse metempsychosis, if one can call it that, that is, to see if this could be their last incarnation as animals, if they were ready to enter a human body in the next life. The experiment succeeded fully, I had three absolutely glaring instances; they left with a psychic being sufficiently conscious to enter a human body. But this is not what men ordinarily do; what they usually do is to spoil the consciousness or rather the instinct of animals.

22 March 1951

Aspiration

The trees aspire for the light. What is this light?

The sun, my child. Have you never seen leaves closing up when night comes, as soon as the sun dips below the horizon?

Can trees have an aspiration for something else?

Something else means what? What are the possible openings for a tree?

To become a man?

A man? But they know nothing about man! As man aspires to be a god?... I knew animals which aspired to become human beings, but they were living with human beings. Cats and dogs, for example, which lived in a close intimacy with human beings, truly had an aspiration. I had a cat which was very, very unhappy for being a cat, it wanted to be a man. It had an untimely death. It used to meditate, it certainly did a kind of sadhana of its own, and when it left, even a portion of its vital being reincarnated in a human being. The little psychic element that was at the centre of the being went directly into a man, but even what was conscious in the vital of the cat went into a human being. But these are rather exceptional cases.

19 August 1953

The Greedy Goat

Animals in their natural state do not ever overeat, they eat according to their hunger and if some food is left over and they do not want it to be eaten by others, they hide it, bury it; they hide it with great care so that they may find it again when they are hungry. But an animal living with man loses this instinct and eats not only all that is given but all that's left within its reach. I lived for some time in a small town in the South of France. There was a grocer there who kept goats and one of them had become quite greedy. He had just received a barrel of molasses — you know what molasses is?... How do you call it here? It is crude sugar, "jaggery". He had received a barrel of jaggery and he opened it — he opened the lid and forgot to put it back. And there it was and the goat was roaming around. The goat thought that it must be quite good since it was left there within its reach! It began to eat it and found it truly excellent. And it went on — as it had lost all its instinct — until literally it fell dead, having eaten too much. Well, a wild animal would never do that. These are the advantages of man's company!

23 September 1953

True Modesty

Generally people pass from an excessive appreciation of their personal value to an equally excessive discouragement. One day they say, "I am wonderful", and the next day, "Oh! I am good for nothing, I can do nothing." That is like a pendulum, isn't it? There is nothing more difficult than knowing exactly what one is; one must neither overrate oneself nor depreciate oneself, but understand one's limits and know how to advance towards the ideal set before oneself. There are people who see in a big way and immediately imagine they can do everything. There are petty officers, for example, who imagine themselves capable of winning all the battles of the world and small people who think they surpass everybody in the world. On the other hand, I have known some people who had abilities but who spent their time thinking, "I am good for nothing." Generally the two extremes are found in the same person. But to find someone who knows exactly where he stands and exactly where he can go, is very rare. We have avoided speaking of vanity because we expect that you won't be filled with vanity as soon as you score a success.

Just imagine, there are plants which are vain! I am speaking of plants one grows for oneself. If one pays them compliments, by words or by feelings, if one admires them, well, they hold up their head — with vanity! It is the same with animals. I am going to tell you a short amusing story.

In Paris there is a garden called "The Garden of Plants": there are animals there also, as well as plants. They had just received a magnificent lion. It was of course in a cage. And it was furious. There was a door in the cage behind which it could hide. And it would hide itself just when the visitors came to see it! I saw that and one day I went up to the cage and began speaking to it (animals are very sensitive to spoken language, they really listen). I began speaking softly to my lion, I said to it, "Oh! how handsome you are, what a pity that you are hiding yourself like this, how much we would like to see you..." Well, it listened. Then, little by little, it looked at me askance, slowly stretched its neck to see me better; later it brought out its paw and, finally, put the tip of its nose against the bars as if saying, "At last, here's someone who understands me!"

11 January 1951

Wiser than Man

I remember a man who came here a very long time ago, to stand as a candidate for the government. It so happened that he was introduced to me because they wanted my opinion of him, and so he asked me questions about the Ashram and the life we lead here, and about what I considered to be an indispensable discipline for life. This man used to smoke the whole day and drank much more than was necessary, and so he complained, you see, that he was often tired and sometimes could not control himself. I told him, "You know, first of all, you must stop smoking and you must stop drinking." He looked at me with an unbelievable bewilderment and said, "But then, if one doesn't either smoke or drink, it is not worth living!" I told him, "If you are still at that stage, it is no use saying anything more."

And this is much more frequent than one thinks. To us it seems absurd, for we have something else which is of course more interesting than smoking and drinking. But for ordinary men the satisfaction of their desires is the very reason for existence. For them it seems to be an affirmation of their independence and their purpose in life. And it is simply a perversion, a deformation which is a denial of the life-instinct, it is an unhealthy interference of thought and vital impulse in physical life. It is an unhealthy impulse which does not usually exist even in animals. In this case, instinct in animals is infinitely more reasonable than human instinct — which, besides, doesn't exist any more, which has been replaced by a very perverted impulse.

Perversion is a human disease, it occurs very rarely in animals, and then only in animals which have come close to man and therefore have been contaminated by his perversion.

There is a story about some officers in North Africa — in Algeria — who had adopted a monkey. The monkey lived with them and one day at dinner they had a grotesque idea and gave the monkey something to drink. They gave it alcohol. The monkey first saw the others drink, this seemed to it something quite interesting, and it drank a glass, a full glass of wine. Afterwards it was ill, as ill as could be, it rolled under the table with all kinds of pains and was really in a very bad condition, that is, it gave the men an example of the spontaneous effect of alcohol when the physical nature is not already perverted. It nearly died of poisoning. It recovered. And some time later it was again allowed to come for dinner as it was all right, and somebody placed a glass of wine in front of it. It picked it up in a terrible rage and flung it at the head of the man who had given the glass... By that it showed that it was much wiser than the men!

It is a good thing to begin to learn at an early age that to lead an efficient life and obtain from one's body the maximum it is able to give, reason must be the master of the house. And it is not a question of yoga or higher realisation, it is something which should be taught everywhere, in every school, every family, every home: man was made to be a mental being, and merely to be a man — we are not speaking of anything else, we are speaking only of being a man — life must be dominated by reason and not by vital impulses. This should be taught to all children from their infancy.

8 May 1957

The Scientist and the Cobra

Why does one feel afraid?

I suppose it is because one is egoistic.

There are three reasons. First, an excessive concern about one's security. Next, what one does not know always gives an uneasy feeling which is translated in the consciousness by fear. And above all, one doesn't have the habit of a spontaneous trust in the Divine....

The first movement of fear comes automatically. There was a great scientist who was also a great psychologist (I don't remember his name now); he had developed his inner consciousness but wanted to test it. So he undertook an experiment. He wanted to know if, by means of consciousness, one could control the reflex actions of the body (probably he didn't go far enough to be able to do it, for it can be done; but in any case, for him it was still impossible). Well, he went to the zoological garden, to the place where snakes were kept in a glass cage. There was a particularly aggressive cobra there; when it was not asleep, it was almost always in a fury, for through the glass it could see people and that irritated it terribly. Our scientist went and stood in front of the cage. He knew very well that it was made in such a way that the snake could never break the glass and that he ran no risk of being attacked. So from there he began to excite the snake by shouts and gestures. The cobra, furious, hurled itself against the glass, and every time it did so the scientist closed his eyes! Our psychologist told himself, "But look here, I know that this snake cannot pass through, why do I close my eyes?" Well, one must recognise that it is difficult to conquer the reaction. It is a sense of protection, and if one feels that one cannot protect oneself, one is afraid. But the movement of fear which is expressed by the eyes fluttering is not a mental or a vital fear: it is a fear in the cells of the body; for it has not been impressed upon them that there is no danger and they do not know how to resist. It is because one has not done yoga, you see. With yoga one can watch with open eyes, one would not close them; but one would not close them because one calls upon something else, and that "something else" is the sense of the divine Presence in oneself which is stronger than everything.

This is the one thing that can cure you of your fear.

14 March 1951

True Courage

I have known people who were physically very courageous, and were very, very cowardly morally, because men are made of different parts. Their physical being can be active and courageous and their moral being cowardly. I have known the opposite also: I have known people who were inwardly very courageous and externally they were terrible cowards. But these have at least the advantage of having an inner will, and even when they tremble they compel themselves.

Once I was asked a question, a psychological question. It was put to me by a man who used to deal in wild animals. He had a menagerie, and he used to buy wild animals everywhere, in all countries where they are caught, in order to sell them again on the European market. He was an Austrian, I think. He had come to Paris, and he said to me, "I have to deal with two kinds of tamers. I would like to know very much which of the two is more courageous. There are those who love animals very much, they love them so much that they enter the cage without the least idea that it could prove dangerous, as a friend enters a friend's house, and they make them work, teach them how to do things, make them work without the slightest fear. I knew some who did not even have a whip in their hands; they went in and spoke with such friendliness to their animals that all went off well. This did not prevent their being eaten up one day.

But still — this is one kind. The other sort are those who are so afraid before entering, that they tremble, you know, generally it makes them sick. But they make an effort, they make a considerable moral effort, and without showing any fear they enter and make the animals work."

Then he told me, "I have heard two opinions: some say that it is much more courageous to overcome fear than not to have any fear... Here's the problem. So which of the two is truly courageous?"

There is perhaps a third kind, which is truly courageous, still more courageous than either of the two. It is the one who is perfectly aware of the danger, who knows very well that one can't trust these animals. The day they are in a particularly excited state they can very well jump on you treacherously. But that's all the same to them. They go there for the joy of the work to be done, without questioning whether there will be an accident or not and in full quietude of mind, with all the necessary force and required consciousness in the body. This indeed was the case of that man himself. He had so terrific a will that without a whip, simply by the persistence of his will, he made them do all that he wanted. But he knew very well that it was a dangerous profession. He had no illusion about it. He told me that he had learnt this work with a cat — a cat!

He was a man who, apart from his work as a trader in wild animals, was an artist. He loved to draw, loved painting, and he had a cat in his studio. And it was in this way that he got interested in animals. This cat was an extremely independent one, and had no sense of obedience. Well, he wanted to make a portrait of his cat. He put it on a chair and went to sit down at his easel. Frrr... the cat ran away. So he went to look for it, took it back, put it back on the chair without even raising his voice, without scolding it, without saying anything to it, without hurting it of course or striking it. He took it up and put it back on the chair. Now, the cat became more and more clever. In the studio in some nooks there were canvasses, canvasses on which one paints, which were hidden and piled on one another, behind, in the corners. So the cat went and sat there behind them. It knew that its master would take some time to bring out all those canvasses and catch it; the man, quietly, took them out one by one, caught the cat and put it back in its place.

He told me that once from sunrise to sunset he did this without stopping. He did not eat, the cat did not eat (*laughter*), he did that the whole day through; at the end of the day it was conquered. When its master put it on the chair it remained there (*laughter*) and from that time onwards it never again tried to run away. Then he told himself, "Why not try the same thing with the bigger animals?" He tried and succeeded.

Of course he couldn't take a lion in this way and put it on a chair, no, but he wanted to get them to make movements — silly ones, indeed, such as are made in circuses: putting their forefeet on a stool, or sitting down with all four paws together on a very small place, all kinds of stupid things, but still that's the fashion, that's what one likes to show; or perhaps to stand up like a dog on the hind legs; or even to roar — when a finger is held up before it, it begins to roar — you see, things like that, altogether stupid. It would be much better to let the animals go round freely, that would be much more interesting. However, as I said, that's the fashion.

But he managed this without any whipping, he never had a pistol in his pocket, and he went in there completely conscious that one day when they were not satisfied they could give him the decisive blow. But he did it quietly and with the same patience as with the cat. And when he delivered his animals — he gave his animals to the circuses, you see, to the tamers — they were wonderful.

Of course, those animals — all animals — feel it if one is afraid, even if one doesn't show it. They feel it extraordinarily, with an instinct which human beings don't have. They feel that you are afraid, your body produces a vibration which arouses an extremely unpleasant sensation in them. If they are strong animals this makes them furious; if they are weak animals, this gives them a panic. But if you have no fear at all, you see, if you go with an absolute trustfulness, a great trust, if you go in a friendly way to them, you will see that they have no fear; they are not afraid, they do not fear you and don't detest you; also, they are very trusting.

It is not to encourage you to enter the cages of all the lions you go to see, but still it is like that. When you meet a barking dog, if you are afraid, it will bite you, if you aren't, it will go away. But you must really not be afraid, not only appear unafraid, because it is not the appearance but the vibration that counts.

26 January 1955

The Subtle Body

Illnesses enter through the subtle body, don't they? How can they be stopped?

Ah! here we are... If one is very sensitive, very sensitive — one must be very sensitive — the moment they touch the subtle body and try to pass through, one feels it. It is not like something touching the body, it is a sort of feeling.... You can become quite conscious of this envelope, and if you develop it sufficiently, you don't even need to look and see, you feel that something has touched you. I can give you an instance of this, there are many similar ones.

Someone was seeking to establish a constant and conscious contact — absolutely constant and conscious — with the inner Godhead, not only with the psychic being but the divine Presence in the psychic being, and she had decided that she would be like this, that she would busy herself with nothing else, that is to say, whatever she might be doing, her concentration was upon this, and even when she went out walking in the street, her concentration was upon this. She lived in a big city where there was much traffic: buses, tramways, etc., many things, and to cross the street one had to be considerably careful, wide-awake and attentive, otherwise one could get run over, but this person had resolved that she would not come out of her concentration. One day when she was crossing one of the big avenues with all its cars and its tramways, still deep in her concentration, in her inner seeking, she suddenly felt at about an arm's length a little shock, like this; she jumped back and a car passed just by her side. If she had not jumped back she would have been run over... This is an extreme point, but without going so far one can very easily feel a kind of little discomfort (it is not something which is imposed with a great force), a little uneasiness coming near you from anywhere at all: front, behind, above, below. If at that moment you are sufficiently alert, you say "no", as though you were cutting off the contact with great strength, and it is finished. If you are not conscious at that moment, the next minute or a few minutes later you get a queer sick feeling inside, a cold in the back, a little uneasiness, the beginning of some disharmony; you feel a maladjustment somewhere, as though the general harmony had been disturbed. Then you must concentrate all the more and with a great strength of will keep the faith that nothing can do you harm, nothing can touch you. This suffices, you can throw off the illness at that moment. But you must do this immediately, you understand, you must not wait for five minutes, it must be done at once. If you wait too long and begin to feel really an uneasiness somewhere, and something begins to get quite disturbed, then it is good to sit down, concentrate and call the Force, concentrate it on the place which is getting disturbed, that is to say, which is beginning to become ill. But if you don't do anything at all, an illness indeed gets lodged somewhere; and all this, because you were not sufficiently alert. And sometimes one is obliged to follow the entire curve to find the favourable moment again and get rid of the business. I have said somewhere that in the physical domain all is a question of method — a method is necessary for realising everything. And if the illness has succeeded in touching the physical-physical, well, you must follow the procedure needed to get rid of it. This is what medical science calls "the course of the illness". One can hasten the course with the help of spiritual forces, but all the same the procedure must be followed. There are some four different stages. The very first is instantaneous. The second can be done in some minutes, the third may take several hours and the fourth several days. And then, once the thing is lodged there, all will depend not only on the receptivity of the body but still more on the willingness of the part which is the cause of the disorder. You know, when the thing comes from outside it is in affinity with something inside. If it manages to pass through, to enter without one's being aware of it, it means there is some affinity somewhere, and the part of the being which has responded must be convinced.

31 March 1951

The Power of Imagination

Imagination is really the power of mental formation. When this power is put at the service of the Divine, it is not only formative but also creative. There is, however, no such thing as an unreal formation, because every image is a reality on the mental plane. The plot of a novel, for instance, is all there on the mental plane existing independently of the physical. Each of us is a novelist to a certain extent and possesses the capacity to make forms on that plane; and, in fact, a good deal of our life embodies the products of our imagination. Every time you indulge your imagination in an unhealthy way, giving a form to your fears and anticipating accidents and misfortunes, you are undermining your own future. On the other hand, the more optimistic your imagination, the greater the chance of your realising your aim. Monsieur Coué got hold of this potent truth and cured hundreds of people by simply teaching them to imagine themselves out of misery. He once related the case of a lady whose hair was falling off. She began to suggest to herself that she was improving every day and that her hair was surely growing. By constantly imagining it her hair really began to grow and even reached an enviable length owing to still further auto-suggestion. The power of mental formation is most useful in Yoga also... Therefore I say to you, never be dejected and disappointed but let your imagination be always hopeful and joyously plastic to the stress of the higher Truth, so that the latter may find you full of the necessary formations to hold its creative light.

Imagination is like a knife which may be used for good or evil purposes. If you always dwell in the idea and feeling that you are going to be transformed, then you will help the process of the Yoga.... In other words, let your imagination be moulded by your faith in Sri Aurobindo; for, is not such faith the very hope and conviction that the will of Sri Aurobindo is bound to be done, that his work of transformation cannot but end in a supreme victory and that what he calls the supramental world will be brought down on earth and realised by us here and now?

1930-1931

Optimism à la Coué

Sweet Mother, what does "optimism à la Coué" mean?

Ah! Coué. You don't know the story of Coué? Coué was a doctor. He used to treat by psychological treatment, auto-suggestion, and he called this the true working of the imagination; and what he defined as imagination was faith. And so he treated all his patients in this way: they had to make a kind of imaginative formation which consisted in thinking themselves cured or in any case on the way to being cured, and in repeating this formation to themselves with sufficient persistence for it to have its effect. He had very remarkable results. He cured lots of people; only, he failed also, and perhaps these were not very lasting cures, I don't know this. But in any case, this made many people reflect on something that's quite true and of capital importance: that the mind is a formative instrument and that if one knows how to use it in the right way, one gets a good result. He observed — and I think it is true, my observation agrees with his — that people spend their time thinking wrongly. Their mental activity is almost always half pessimistic, and even half destructive. They are all the time thinking of and foreseeing bad things which may happen, troublesome consequences of what they have done, and they construct all kinds of catastrophes with an exuberant imagination which, if it were utilised in the other way, would naturally have opposite and more satisfying results.

If you observe yourself, if you... how to put it?... if you catch yourself thinking — well, if you do it suddenly, if you look at yourself thinking all of a sudden, spontaneously, unexpectedly, you will notice that nine times out of ten you are thinking something troublesome. It is very rarely that you are thinking about harmonious, beautiful, constructive, happy things, full of hope, light and joy; you will see, try the experiment.

...You will notice this: that you act, you do all that you have to do, without having a single thought about your body, and when all of a sudden you wonder whether there isn't anything that's going wrong, whether there is some uneasiness or a difficulty, something, then you begin to think of your body and you think about it with anxiety and begin to make your disastrous constructions.

Whereas Coué recommended... It was in this way that he cured his patients; he was a doctor, he told them, "You are going to repeat to yourself: 'I am being cured, gradually I am getting cured' and again, you see, 'I am strong, I am quite healthy and I can do this, I can do that'."

I knew someone who was losing her hair disastrously, by handfuls. She was made to try this method. When combing her hair she made herself think, "My hair will not fall out." The first and second time it did not work, but she continued and each time before combing the hair she used to repeat with insistence, "I am going to comb my hair but it won't fall out."

And within a month her hair stopped falling. Later she again continued thinking, "Now my hair will grow." And she succeeded so well that I saw her with magnificent hair, and it was she herself who told me this, that this was what she had done after being on the point of becoming bald. It is very, very effective. Only, while one is making the formation, another part of the mind must not say, "Oh, I am making a formation and it is not going to be successful", because in this way you undo your own work.

Coué — it was at the beginning of the century, I think... (*Mother turns to Pavitra.*)

> (Pavitra) *I saw him in 1917 or 1918 in Paris.*

Yes, that's right, the beginning of the century, the first quarter of the century. You knew him?

> (Pavitra) *In Paris, yes.*

Ah ah! tell us about it.

> (Pavitra) *I heard one or two of his lectures. The method he gave to the sick was to repeat, first every morning and several times a day, "I am becoming better and better, every day I am better and better, each day I am healthier", every morning, every evening, several times a day, with conviction, clasping the hands like this...*

Oh! if one lost one's temper: "I am becoming better and better, I don't lose my temper now." (*Laughter*)

(Pavitra) *"Every day I am becoming more and more intelligent."*

That's really good. Why, and if you repeat to a child, if you make him repeat, "I am good, day by day more and more."

"I am better and better, I am more and more obedient." Oh, but this is very fine. (*To a teacher*) The other day you wanted to know what to do for children who are difficult to bring up. Here you are, you can try this. "I am more and more regular at school."

And then again, "I don't tell lies any more. I shall never lie again."

(Pavitra) *At first it was to be said in the future and then one drew closer to the present, and so finished in the present itself.*

Oh, one finishes in the present. And how long did it take?

(Pavitra) *It depended on the person.*

It depends on the case, "I shall not tell lies again, it is my last lie." (*Laughter*)

5 January 1955

One Grape Every Two Steps

Every doctor who is something of a philosopher will tell you: "It is like that; we doctors give only the occasion, but it is the body that cures itself. When the body wants to be cured, it is cured." Well, there are bodies that do not allow equilibrium to be reestablished unless thay are made to absorb some medicine or something very definite which gives them the feeling that they are being truly looked after. But if you give them a very precise, very exact treatment that is sometimes very difficult to follow, they begin to be convinced that there is nothing better to do than to regain the equilibrium and they get back the equilibrium!

I knew a doctor who was a neurologist and treated illnesses of the stomach. He used to say that all illness of the stomach came from a more or less bad nervous state. He was a doctor for the rich and it was the rich and unoccupied people who went to him. So they used to come and tell him: "I have a pain in the stomach, I cannot digest", and this and that. They had terrible pains, they had headache, they had, well, all the symptoms! He used to listen to them very seriously. I knew a lady who went to him and to whom he said: "Ah! your case is very serious. But on which floor do you live? On the ground floor? All right. This is what you have to do to cure your illness of the stomach. Take a bunch of fully ripe grapes (do not take your breakfast, for breakfast upsets your stomach), take a bunch of grapes; hold it in your hand, like this, very carefully. Then prepare to go out — not by your door, never go out by your door! You must go out by the window. Get a stool. And go out by the window. Go out in the street, and there you must walk while eating one grape every two steps — not more, yes, not more! You will have stomach-ache! One single grape every two steps. You must take two steps, then eat one single grape and you should continue till there are no more grapes. Do not turn back, go straight on till there are no more grapes. You must take a big bunch. And when you have finished, you may return quietly. But do not take a conveyance! Come back on foot, otherwise the whole trouble will return. Come back quietly and I give you the guarantee that if you do that everyday, at the end of three days you will be cured." And in fact this lady was cured!

24 June 1953

Food for a Nightmare

What happens if one eats meat?

Do you want me to tell you a story? I knew a lady, a young Swedish woman, who was doing sadhana; and she was by habit a vegetarian, by choice and by habit. One day she was invited by some friends who gave her chicken for dinner. She did not want to make a fuss, she ate the chicken. But afterwards, during the night suddenly she found herself in a basket with her head between two pieces of wicker-work, shaken, shaken, shaken, and feeling wretched, miserable; and then, after that she found herself head down, feet in the air, and being shaken, shaken, shaken. (*Laughter*) She felt perfectly miserable; and then all of a sudden, somebody began pulling out things from her body, and that hurt her terribly, and then someone came along with a knife and chopped off her head; and then she woke up. She told me all this; she said she had never had such a frightful nightmare, that she had not thought of anything before going to sleep, that it was just the consciousness of the poor chicken that had entered her, and that she had experienced in her dream all the anguish the poor chicken had suffered when it was carried to the market, sold, its feathers plucked and its neck cut! (*Laughter*)

That's what happens! That is to say, in a greater or lesser proportion you swallow along with the meat a little of the consciousness of the animal you eat. It is not very serious, but it is not always very pleasant. And obviously it does not help you in being on the side of man rather than of the beast!... For an ordinary man, living an ordinary life, having ordinary activities, not thinking at all of anything else except earning his living, of keeping himself fit and perhaps taking care of his family, it is good to eat meat, it is all right for him to eat anything at all, whatever agrees with him, whatever does him good.

But if one wishes to pass from this ordinary life to a higher one, the problem begins to become interesting; and if, after having come to a higher life, one tries to prepare oneself for the transformation, then it becomes very important. For there certainly are foods which help the body to become subtle and others which keep it in a state of animality.

23 June 1954

Friendship with the Sun

I knew young people who had always lived in cities — in a city and in those little rooms one has in the big cities in which everyone is huddled. Now, they had come to spend their holidays in the countryside, in the south of France, and there the sun is hot, naturally not as here but all the same it is very hot (when we compare the sun of the Mediterranean coasts with that of Paris, for example, it truly makes a difference), and so, when they walked around the countryside the first few days they really began to get a terrible headache and to feel absolutely uneasy because of the sun; but they suddenly thought: "Why, if we make friends with the sun it won't harm us any more!" And they began to make a kind of inner effort of friendship and trust in the sun, and when they were out in the sun, instead of trying to bend double and tell themselves, "Oh! how hot it is, how it burns!", they said, "Oh, how full of force and joy and love the sun!" etc., they opened themselves like this (*gesture*), and not only did they not suffer any longer but they felt so strong afterwards that they went round telling everyone who said "It is hot" — telling them, "Do as we do, you will see how good it is." And they could remain for hours in the full sun, bare-headed and without feeling any discomfort. It is the same principle.

It is the same principle. They linked themselves to the universal vital force which is in the sun and received this force which took away all that was unpleasant to them.

When one is in the countryside, when one walks under the trees and feels so close to Nature, to the trees, the sky, all the leaves, all the branches, all the herbs, when one feels a great friendship with these things and breathes that air which is so good, perfumed with all the plants, then one opens oneself, and by opening oneself communes with the universal forces. And for all things it is like that!

4 May 1955

Shooting Star

Sweet Mother, it is said that if one sees a shooting star and at that moment one aspires for something, that aspiration is fulfilled within the year. Is this true?

Do you know what that means? The aspiration must be formulated during the time the star is visible; and that doesn't last long, does it? Well, if an aspiration can be formulated while the star is visible, this means that it is all the time *there, present,* in the forefront of the consciousness — this does not apply to ordinary things, it has nothing to do with that, it concerns a spiritual aspiration. But the point is that if you are able to articulate your spiritual aspiration just at that moment, it means that it is right in front of your consciousness, that it dominates your consciousness. And, necessarily, what dominates your consciousness can be realised very swiftly.

I had the opportunity to make this experiment. Exactly this. The moment the star was passing, at that very moment there sprang up from the consciousness: "To realise the divine union, for my body." That very moment.

And before the end of the year, it was done.

But it was not because of the star! It was because that dominated my whole consciousness and I was thinking of nothing but that, I wanted only that, thought only of that, acted only for that. So, this thing which generally takes a whole lifetime — it is said the minimum time is thirty-five years! — before twelve months had passed, it was done.

But that was because I thought only of that.

And it was because I was thinking only of that, that just when the star flashed by I could formulate it — not merely a vague impression — formulate it in precise words like this: "To realise union with the Divine", the inner Divine, the thing we speak of, the very thing we speak of.

Therefore, what is important is not the star but the aspiration. The star is only like an outer demonstration, nothing else. But it is not necessary to have a shooting star in order to realise swiftly! What is necessary is that the whole will of the being should be concentrated on one point.

4 July 1956

Child Prodigies

Recently, in one of the Wednesday classes, we talked about child prodigies. Some say that the number of child prodigies is increasing considerably, and some — even among Americans — say it is the influence and work of Sri Aurobindo, and others say it is a result of atom bombs! But the fact is that there is a fairly large number of child prodigies. I did not want to speak about it in much detail, for I did not have any proofs in hand, that is, I did not have any good examples to give. It happens that since then someone has brought me a French book written by a child of eight.[1] Naturally there are people who dispute the possibility, but I shall explain to you later how such a thing is possible.

The book is remarkable for a child of eight. This does not mean that if the age of the child were not known the book would be considered wonderful; but there are, here and there, some sentences in it which are quite astonishing. I have noted down these sentences and am going to read them out to you. (*Mother skims through her book.*)

A little phrase like this: "If we truly love one another, we can hide nothing from each other"... Obviously this is fine.

And then something else written to a boy with freckles — you know what freckles are, don't you?

1. Minou Drouet, born in 1947, author of *Arbre mon ami*.

She writes to him: "You are beautiful, yes indeed, your freckles are so pretty; one would say that an angel had sown grains of wheat all over your face so as to attract the birds of the sky there." Surely this is very poetic.

And finally, something really fine which opens the door to the explanation I am going to give you: "I am only an ear, a mouth; the ear hears a storm of words which I cannot explain to you, which an immense voice hurls within me, and my mouth repeats them and nothing of what I say can compare with the streaming of light which is within me."

Obviously this is very beautiful.

It seems that here and there in her poems — she has written many — one can find reminiscences of Maeterlinck, for instance; so people have concluded that it was not she who had written them, for at the age of eight one doesn't read Maeterlinck, that it must have been someone else. But in fact there is no need at all to suppose a hoax, and the publisher indeed declares that he is sure of what he is about, that he knows the child very intimately — in fact he was in a way her adoptive father, for her father was dead — and can guarantee that there is no deception. But it is not at all necessary to suppose a deception in order to explain this phenomenon.

Authors, writers, who were inspired and serious in their creative work, that is to say, who were concentrated in a kind of consecration of their being to their literary work, form within themselves a sort of mental entity extremely well-constituted and coordinated, having its own life, *independent of the body,* so that when they die, when the body returns to the earth, this mental formation continues to exist altogether autonomously and independently, and as it has been fashioned for expression it always seeks a means of expression somewhere. And if there happens to be a child who has been formed in particularly favourable circumstances — for instance, the mother of this little girl is herself a poetess and a writer; perhaps the mother herself had an aspiration, a wish that her child would be a remarkable, exceptional being — anyway, if the child who is conceived is formed in particularly favourable circumstances, an entity of this kind may enter into the child at the time of birth and try to use him to express itself; and in that case, this gives a maturity to the child's mind, which is quite extraordinary, exceptional and which enables him to do things of the kind we have just read.

We could say, without fear of sounding quite absurd, that if what she has written surprisingly resembles certain things in Maeterlinck or has the characteristics of his writings, even with certain almost identical turns of phrase, we could very well imagine that a mental formation of Maeterlinck has incarnated in this child and is using this young instrument to express itself.

There are similar examples, for instance, among musicians. There are pianists who have individualised their hands and made them so wonderfully conscious that these hands are not decomposed — not the physical hands: the hands of the subtle physical and vital — they are not decomposed, do not dissolve at the time of death. They remain as instruments to play the piano and always try to incarnate in the hands of someone playing the piano. I have known some cases of people who, as they were about to play, felt as though other hands entered into theirs and started playing really marvellously, in a way they could not have done themselves.

These things are not as exceptional as one might believe, they happen quite often.

I saw the same thing in someone who used to play the violin and another who played the cello — two different cases — and who were not very wonderful performers themselves. One of them was just beginning his studies and the other was a good performer, but nothing marvellous. But all of a sudden, the moment they played the compositions of certain musicians, something of that musician entered into their hands and made their performance absolutely wonderful.

There was even a person — a woman — who used to play the Cello, and the moment she played Beethoven, the expression of her face completely changed into Beethoven's and what she played was sublime, which she could not have played unless something of Beethoven's mind had entered into her.

3 October 1956

Flowers Are Extremely Receptive

Flowers are extremely receptive. All the flowers to which I have given a significance receive exactly the force I put into them and transmit it. People don't always receive it because most of the time they are less receptive than the flower, and they waste the force that has been put in it through their unconsciousness and lack of receptivity. But the force is there, and the flower receives it wonderfully.

I knew this a very long time ago... fifty years ago. There was that occultist who later gave me lessons in occultism for two years. His wife was a wonderful clairvoyant and had an absolutely remarkable capacity — precisely — of transmitting forces. They lived in Tlemcen. I was in Paris. I used to correspond with them. I had not yet met them at all. And then, one day, she sent me in a letter petals of the pomegranate flower, "Divine's Love". At that time I had not given the meaning to the flower. She sent me petals of pomegranate flowers telling me that these petals were bringing her protection and force.

Now, at that time I used to wear my watch on a chain. Wrist-watches were not known then or there were very few. And there was also a small eighteenth century magnifying-glass... it was quite small, as large as this (*gesture*). And it had two lenses, you see, like all reading-glasses; there were two lenses mounted on a small golden frame, and it was hanging from my chain. Now, between the two glasses I put these petals and I used to carry this about with me always because I wanted to keep it with me; you see, I trusted this lady and knew she had power. I wanted to keep this with me, and I always felt a kind of energy, warmth, confidence, force which came from that thing... I did not think about it, you see, but I felt it like that.

And then, one day, suddenly I felt quite depleted, as though a support that was there had gone. Something very unpleasant. I said, "It is strange; what has happened? Nothing really unpleasant has happened to me. Why do I feel like this, so empty, emptied of energy?" And in the evening, when I took off my watch and chain, I noticed that one of the small glasses had come off and all the petals were gone. There was not one petal left. Then I really knew that they carried a considerable charge of power, for I had felt the difference without even knowing the reason. I didn't know the reason and yet it had made a considerable difference. So it was after this that I saw how one could use flowers by charging them with forces. They are extremely receptive.

14 July 1954

Mother in Tokyo in 1916

Six Hundred Vegetables

The number of plants... nobody has ever known and nobody will probably ever know the number of different plants there are upon earth. Yet when a list is made of the number of plants men know and use, it is ridiculously small. I believe, when I was in Japan, the Japanese used to tell me that Europeans eat only three hundred and fifty types of different plants, whilst they use more than six hundred. That makes a considerable difference. They used to say: "Oh, how you waste your food! Nature produces infinitely more than you know; you waste all that." Have you ever eaten (not here, but in Europe) bamboo sprouts?... You have eaten bamboo sprouts? You have eaten palm-tree buds? Coconut buds? — That, indeed, makes a marvellous salad, coconut buds. Only, this kills the tree. For a salad, one kills a tree. But when there is a cyclone, for instance, which knocks down hundreds of coconut trees, the only way of utilising the catastrophe is to eat all the buds and make yourself a magnificent dish. Haven't you ever eaten coconut buds? As for me, I was not surprised, for I had eaten bamboo sprouts before they sprang up from the ground — somewhat like the asparagus. It is quite a classical dish in Japan. And their bamboos are much more tender than the bamboos here. Their bamboos are very tender and their sprouts are wonderful.

Still, that's how it is. It seems in Europe one knows how to use only three hundred and fifty varieties of vegetables from the vegetable kingdom, whilst in Japan they use six hundred of them and more. But perhaps if people knew, they would not die of hunger, at least those who live in the countryside. *Voilà.*

18 November 1953

Vegetables Speak

In Tokyo I had a garden and in this garden I was growing vegetables myself. I had a fairly big garden and many vegetables. And so, every morning I used to go for a walk, after having watered them and so on; I used to walk around to choose which vegetables I could take for eating. Well, just imagine! there were some which said to me, "No, no, no, no, no."... And then there were others which called, and I saw them from a distance, and they were saying, "Take me, take me, take me!" So it was very simple, I looked for those which wanted to be taken and never did I touch those which did not. I used to think it was something exceptional. I loved my plants very much, I used to look after them, I had put a lot of consciousness into them while watering them, cleaning them, so I thought they had a special capacity, perhaps.

But in France it was the same thing. I had a garden also in the south of France where I used to grow peas, radishes, carrots. Well, there were some which were happy, which asked to be taken and eaten, and there were those which said, "No, no, no, don't touch me, don't touch me!" (*Laughter*)

Why did they say that, Sweet Mother?

Well, I experimented precisely to find out; and the result was not always the same. At times it was indeed that the plant was not edible; it was not good, it was hard or bitter, it was not good for eating. At other times it happened that it was not ready, that it was too early; it wasn't ripe. By waiting for a day or two, a day or two later it said to me, "Take me, take me, take me!" (*Laughter*)

23 June 1954

Think in the Stomach

In "The Brain of India" Sri Aurobindo has written that the Bengalis can think with their hearts...

Who can think with his heart?... The Bengalis can think with their hearts? That's a poetic way of saying it. (*Laughter*) Where has he written this? It is indeed a very poetic description. That's to say that they are essentially emotive beings, and that their heart is conscious even in their thought, that their thought is not purely intellectual and dry, and that their heart is aware of their thought. That's what he meant.

But I can also tell you that when I was in Japan I met a man who had formed a group, for... It can't be said that it was for sadhana, but for a kind of discipline. He had a theory and it was on this theory that he had founded his group: that one can think in any part of one's being whatever if one concentrates there. That is to say, instead of thinking in your head, you can think in your chest. And he said that one could think here (*gesture*) in the stomach. He took the stomach as the seat of *prâna*, you see, that is, the vital force. He used certain Sanskrit words, you know, half-digested, and all that.... But still, this does not matter, he was full of good will and he said that most human miseries come from the fact that men think in their heads, that this makes the head ache, tires you and takes away your mental clarity. On the other hand, if you learn how to think here (*gesture indicating the stomach*), it gives you power, strength and calmness. And the most remarkable thing is that he had attained a kind of ability to bring down the mental power, the mental force exactly here (*gesture*); the mental activity was generated there, and no longer in the head. And he had cured a considerable number of people, considerable, some hundreds, who used to suffer from terrible headaches; he had cured them in this way.

I have tried it, it is quite easy, precisely because, as I told you a while ago, the mental force, mental activity is independent of the brain. We are in the habit of using the brain but we can use something else or rather, concentrate the mental force elsewhere, and have the impression that our mental activity comes from there. One can concentrate one's mental force in the solar plexus, here (*gesture*), and feel the mental activity coming out from there.

That man used to say, "Haven't you noticed that all men who have great power have a big belly? (*Laughter*) — Because they concentrate their forces there, so this makes their stomach big!" He always used to give the example of Napoleon; and he said, "These people stand up quite straight, always straight with the head erect, never like this (*Mother bends the head forward*), never like this (*Mother bends the head to the right*), never like this (*Mother bends the head to the left*); always quite straight up but with all their force here (*pointing to the stomach*), and so this makes them very powerful!" And he always spoke of Napoleon. He used to say, "Napoleon, you see..." (*Mother shows that Napoleon had a big stomach.*) And he had a visit from Tagore when Tagore was in Japan and he told me, "Have you observed how Tagore stands quite upright, like this, with his head erect?" Then I told him, "But he doesn't have a big stomach!" He said to me, "It will come." (*Laughter*)

There were hundreds of people at his meetings. They would all sit on their knees as one does in Japan. He struck a table with a stick and everyone brought down his mental force to the stomach; and then they remained like that for... oh! at least half an hour. And after half an hour he struck the table a second time and they released their mental force and began chatting... not very much, for the Japanese do not chat much, but nevertheless they talk.

There now! But mark that there was something very true, in the sense that if ever you have a headache I advise you to do this: to take the thought-force, the mental force — and even if you can draw a little of your vital force, that too — and make it come down, like this (*gesture of very slowly sliding both hands from the top of the head downwards*). Well, if you have a headache or a congestion, if you have caught a touch of the sun, for instance, indeed if anything has happened to you, well, if you know how to do this and bring down the force here, like this, here (*showing the centre of the chest*), or even lower down (*showing the stomach*), well, it will disappear.

8 September 1954

Art and Yoga

The discipline of Art has at its centre the same principle as the discipline of Yoga. In both the aim is to become more and more conscious; in both you have to learn to see and feel something that is beyond the ordinary vision and feeling, to go within and bring out from there deeper things. Painters have to follow a discipline for the growth of the consciousness of their eyes, which in itself is almost a Yoga. If they are true artists and try to see beyond and use their art for the expression of the inner world, they grow in consciousness by this concentration, which is not other than the consciousness given by Yoga....

I have known some who had very little training and skill and yet through Yoga acquired a fine capacity in writing and painting. Two examples I can cite to you. One was a girl who had no education whatever; she was a dancer and danced tolerably well. After she took up Yoga, she danced only for friends; but her dancing attained a depth of expression and beauty which was not there before. And although she was not educated, she began to write wonderful things; for she had visions and expressed them in the most beautiful language. But there were ups and downs in her Yoga, and when she was in a good condition, she wrote beautifully, but otherwise was quite dull and stupid and uncreative. The second case is that of a boy who had studied art, but only just a little. The son of a diplomat, he had been trained for the diplomatic career; but he lived in luxury and his studies did not go far. Yet as soon as he took up Yoga, he began to produce inspired drawings which carried the expression of an inner knowledge and were symbolic in character; in the end he became a great artist.

28 July 1929

The Art of Japan

The art of Japan is a kind of directly mental expression in physical life. The Japanese use the vital world very little. Their art is extremely mentalised; their life is extremely mentalised. It expresses in detail quite precise mental formations. Only, in the physical, they have spontaneously the sense of beauty. For example, a thing one sees very rarely in Europe but constantly, daily in Japan: very simple people, men of the working class or even peasants go for rest or enjoyment to a place where they can see a beautiful landscape. This gives them a much greater joy than going to play cards or indulging in all sorts of distractions as they do in the countries of Europe. They are seen in groups at times, going on the roads or sometimes taking a train or a tram up to a certain point, then walking to a place from where one gets a beautiful view. Then at this place there is a small house which fits very well into the landscape, there is a kind of small platform on which one can sit: one takes a cup of tea and at the same time sees the landscape. For them, this is the supreme enjoyment; they know nothing more pleasant. One can understand this among artists, educated people, quite learned people, but I am speaking of people of the most ordinary class, poor people who like this better than resting or relaxing at home. This is for them the greatest joy.

And in that country, for each season there are known sites. For instance, in autumn leaves become

Mother in Japan

Drawings by Mother during her stay in Japan

red; they have large numbers of maple-trees (the leaves of the maple turn into all the shades of the most vivid red in autumn, it is absolutely marvellous), so they arrange a place near a temple, for instance, on the top of a hill, and the entire hill is covered with maples. There is a stairway which climbs straight up, almost like a ladder, from the base to the top, and it is so steep that one cannot see what is at the top, one gets the feeling of a ladder rising to the skies — a stone stairway, very well made, rising steeply and seeming to lose itself in the sky — clouds pass, and both the sides of the hill are covered with maples, and these maples have the most magnificent colours you could ever imagine. Well, an artist who goes there will experience an emotion of absolutely exceptional, marvellous beauty. But one sees very small children, families even, with a baby on the shoulder, going there in groups. In autumn they will go there. In springtime they will go elsewhere.

There is a garden quite close to Tokyo where irises are grown, a garden with very tiny rivulets, and along the rivulets, irises — irises of all possible colours — and it is arranged according to colour, organised in such a way that on entering one is dazzled, there is a blaze of colour from all these flowers standing upright; and there are heaps and heaps of them, as far as the eye can reach. At another time, just at the beginning of spring (it is a slightly early spring there), there are the first cherry-trees. These cherry-trees never give fruit, they are grown only for the flowers. They range from white to pink, to a rather vivid pink. There are long avenues all bordered with cherry-trees, all pink; they are huge trees which have turned all pink. There are entire mountains covered with these cherry-trees, and on the little rivulets bridges have been built which too are all red: you see these bridges of red lacquer among all these pink flowers and, below, a great river flowing and a mountain which seems to scale the sky, and they go to this place in springtime.... For each season there are flowers and for each flower there are gardens.

And people travel by train as easily as one goes from house to house; they have a small packet like this which they carry; in it they have a change of clothes, that's quite enough for them; they wear on the feet rope or fibre sandals; when these get worn out they throw them away and take others, for it costs nothing at all. All their life is like that. They have paper handkerchiefs, when they have used them they get rid of them, and so on — they don't burden themselves with anything. When they go by train, at the station small meals are sold in boxes (it is quite clean, quite neat), small meals in boxes of white wood with little chop-sticks for eating; then, as all this has no value, when one has finished, one puts them aside, doesn't bother about them or encumber oneself. They live like that. When they have a garden or a park, they plant trees, and they plant them just at the place where, when the tree has grown, it will create a landscape, will fit into a landscape. And as they want the tree to have a particular shape, they trim it, cut it, they manage to give it all the shapes they want. You have trees with fantastic forms; they have cut off the unnecessary branches, fostered others, contrived things as they liked. Then you come to a place and you see a house which seems to be altogether a part of the landscape; it has exactly the right colour, it is made of the right materials; it is not like a blow in your face, as are all those European buildings which spoil the whole landscape. It is just there where it should be, hidden under the trees; then you see a creeper and suddenly a wonderful tree: it is there at the right place, it has the right form. I had everything to learn in Japan. For four years, from an artistic point of view, I lived from wonder to wonder.

And in the cities, a city like Tokyo, for example, which is the biggest city in the world, bigger than London, and which extends far, far (now the houses are modernised, the whole centre of the city is very unpleasant, but when I was there, it was still nice), in the outlying parts of the city, those which are not business quarters, every house has at the most two storeys and a garden — there is always a garden, there are always one or two trees which are quite lovely. And then, if you go for a walk... it is very difficult to find your way in Tokyo; there are no straight streets with houses on either side according to the number, and you lose your way easily. Then you go wandering around — always one wanders at random in that country — you go wandering and all of a sudden you turn the corner of a street and come to a kind of paradise: there are magnificent trees, a temple as beautiful as everything else, you see nothing of the city any longer, no more traffic, no tramways; a corner, a corner of trees with magnificent colours, and it is beautiful, truly beautiful. You do not know how you have reached there, you seem to have come by luck. And then you turn, you seek your way, you wander off again and go elsewhere. And some days later you want to come back to this very place, but it is impossible, it is as though it had disappeared. And this is so frequent, this is so true that such stories are often told in Japan. Their literature is full of fairy-lore. They tell you a story in which the hero comes suddenly to an enchanted place: he sees fairies, he sees marvellous beings, he spends exquisite hours among flowers, music; all is splendid. The next day he is obliged to leave; it is the law of the place, he goes away. He tries to come back, but never does. He can no longer find the place: it was there, it has disappeared!... And everything in this city, in this country, from beginning to end, gives you the impression of impermanence, of the unexpected, the exceptional. You always come across things you did not expect; you want to find them again and they are lost — they have made something else which is equally charming. From the artistic point of view, the point of view of beauty, I don't think there is a country as beautiful as that.

12 April 1951

The Woman Who Knew How to Walk

If you want to learn, you can learn at every moment. As for me I have learnt even by listening to little children's chatter. Every moment something may happen; someone may say a word to you, even an idiot may say a word that opens you to something enabling you to make some progress. And you can't imagine how interesting life becomes! You can no longer get bored, that is gone, everything is interesting, everything is wonderful — because every minute you can learn, at each step make progress. For example, when you are in the street, instead of being simply there and not knowing what you are doing, if you look around, if you observe... I remember having been thus obliged to be in the street on a shopping errand or going to see someone or to purchase something, that's not important; indeed, it is not always pleasant to be in the street, but if you begin to observe and to see how this person walks, how that one moves, how this light plays upon that object, how this little bit of a tree there suddenly makes the landscape pretty, how hundreds of things shine... then every minute you can learn something. Not only can you learn, but I remember to have once had — I was just walking in the street — to have had a kind of illumination, because there was a woman walking in front of me and truly she knew how to walk. How lovely it was! Her movement was magnificent! I saw that and suddenly I saw the whole origin of Greek culture, how all these forms descend towards the world to express Beauty — simply because here was a woman who knew how to walk! You understand, this is how all things become interesting. And so, instead of going to the class and doing stupid things there (I hope none of you does that, I am sure all who come here to my class will never go and do stupid things at school, that it is exceptions that prove the rule; however, I know that unfortunately too many go there and do all the idiotic things one might invent), so, instead of that, if you could go to the class in order to make progress, every day a new little progress — even if it be the understanding why your teacher bores you — it would be wonderful, for all of a sudden he will no longer be boring to you, all of a sudden you will discover that he is very interesting! It is like that. If you look at life in this way, life becomes something wonderful. That is the only way of making it interesting, because life upon earth is made to be a field for progress and if we progress to the maximum we draw the maximum benefit from our life upon earth. And then one feels happy. When one does the best one can, one is happy.

13 May 1953

How Mother Works in Our Consciousness

Each one has his own little world... of mental formations of which some are clothed in vital substance, and all these crawl together, mix with each other, knock against each other. There is a struggle to see which is the strongest, which tries to realise itself, and all this creates an atmosphere indeed!...

When you come to me, it is all this I see. It is exactly this I see, and that is why your coming is useful. Because, to give you a flower is of course very nice, but that's not anything much... there are things more important than that. But every time I see you, in a second — a flash is enough, a second — each one who comes appears with all his formations, and then I do just... I do just this... (*gesture*). The flower is an excuse, through the flower I give something.

And then, when sometimes, you know, I seem to go deep within, my eyes close, and then very slowly either I give something or I don't move for a moment — that's when the work to be done is urgent. Sometimes it is necessary to intervene for one reason or another, to help or to demolish something, or to push you towards some progress which is beginning, or other things like that... So I just catch hold of your hand sometimes, you see: "Don't move!" So the person thinks: "Mother has gone into a trance." I feel quite amused... (*Laughter*) I am busy working, putting things in order; sometimes I am obliged to perform a surgical operation, I take away certain things which are there and should not be there. A second is enough, you see, I don't need any time for this; sometimes the work takes a little longer, a few more seconds, a minute... Otherwise, usually — in a general way — when things are as we would say "normal", it is enough just to see, you understand, and... the response! I give the flower... even without the flower, like this... simply I put just the little flash or sometimes the little red-hot iron, or a light, anything, and just at the right moment and the right place where it is needed... *Au revoir*!

11 August 1954

Tiger Becomes... Tiny Little Cat!

I practised occultism when I was twelve. But I must say I had no fear, I feared nothing. One goes out of one's body, but is tied by something resembling an almost imperceptible thread; if the thread is cut, it is all over. Life also is ended. One goes out, and then can begin seeing the world he has entered. And usually the first things one sees, as I said, are terrifying. Because, for you the air is empty, there is nothing in it — you see something blue or white, there are clouds, sunbeams, and all that is very pretty — but when you have the other sight, you see that it is filled with a multitude of small formations which are all residues of desires or of mental deformations and these swarm inside it, you see, in a mass, and this is not always very pretty. At times it is extremely ugly. This assails you; it comes, presses upon you, attacks you; and if you are afraid, it takes absolutely frightful forms. Naturally, if you do not flinch, if you can look upon all that with a healthy curiosity, you perceive that it is not at all so terrifying. It may not be pretty, but it is not terrifying.

I could tell you a little story.

I knew a Danish painter who was quite talented and who wanted to learn occultism. He had come here, you know, had met Sri Aurobindo; he had even done his portrait. That was during the war, and when he came back to France, he wanted me to teach him a little of this occult science. I taught him how to go out of his body etc., and the controls, all that. And I told him that, above all, the first thing was not to have any fear. Then, one day he came to tell me that he had had a dream the night before. But it was not a dream, for, as I have told you, he knew a bit about how to go out of his body, and he had gone out consciously. And once he had gone out he was looking around seeing what was to be seen, when suddenly he saw a formidable tiger coming towards him, drawing close with the most frightful intentions... He remembered what I had told him, that he must not be afraid. So he began to say to himself, "There is no danger, I am protected, nothing can happen to me, I am wrapped up in the power of protection", and he began looking at the tiger in that way, without any fear. And as he went on looking at the tiger, immediately it began to grow smaller and smaller and smaller and — it became a tiny little cat! (*Laughter*)

What does the tiger represent?

It was probably... That day he had become angry with somebody, he had lost his temper and entertained bad thoughts; he had hoped that something very unpleasant would happen to this person. Now, in occultism there is the "rebound". You send out a bad thought, it returns to you as an attack. That is exactly one of the reasons why you must have a complete control over your feelings, sensations, thoughts, for if you become angry with someone or think badly of him, or if, still worse, you wish him ill, well, in your very dream you see this person coming with an extreme violence to attack you. Then, if you do not know these things, you say, "Why, I was right in having bad thoughts against him!" But in fact, it is not at all that. It is your own thought that comes back to you.

3 March 1954

Alexandra David-Neel and Mr. Tiger

A Buddhist story

As I am still unable to read to you this evening, I am going to tell you a story. It is a Buddhist story which perhaps you know, it is modern but has the merit of being authentic. I heard it from Alexandra David-Neel who, as you probably know, is a well-known Buddhist, especially as she was the first European woman to enter Lhasa. Her journey to Tibet was very perilous and thrilling and she narrated one of the incidents of this journey to me, which I am going to tell you this evening.

She was with a certain number of fellow travellers forming a sort of caravan, and as the approach to Tibet was relatively easier through Indo-China, they were going from that side. Indo-China is covered with large forests, and these forests are infested with tigers, some of which become man-eaters... and when that happens they are called: "Mr. Tiger."

Late one evening, when they were in the thick of the forest — a forest they had to cross in order to be able to camp safely — she realised that it was her meditation hour. Now, she used to meditate at fixed times, very regularly, without ever missing one and as it was time for her meditation she told her companions, "Carry on, I shall sit here and do my meditation, and when I have finished I shall join you; meanwhile, go

Mother giving dictation to children of the Green Group in the Guest House courtyard at the Playground in 1951

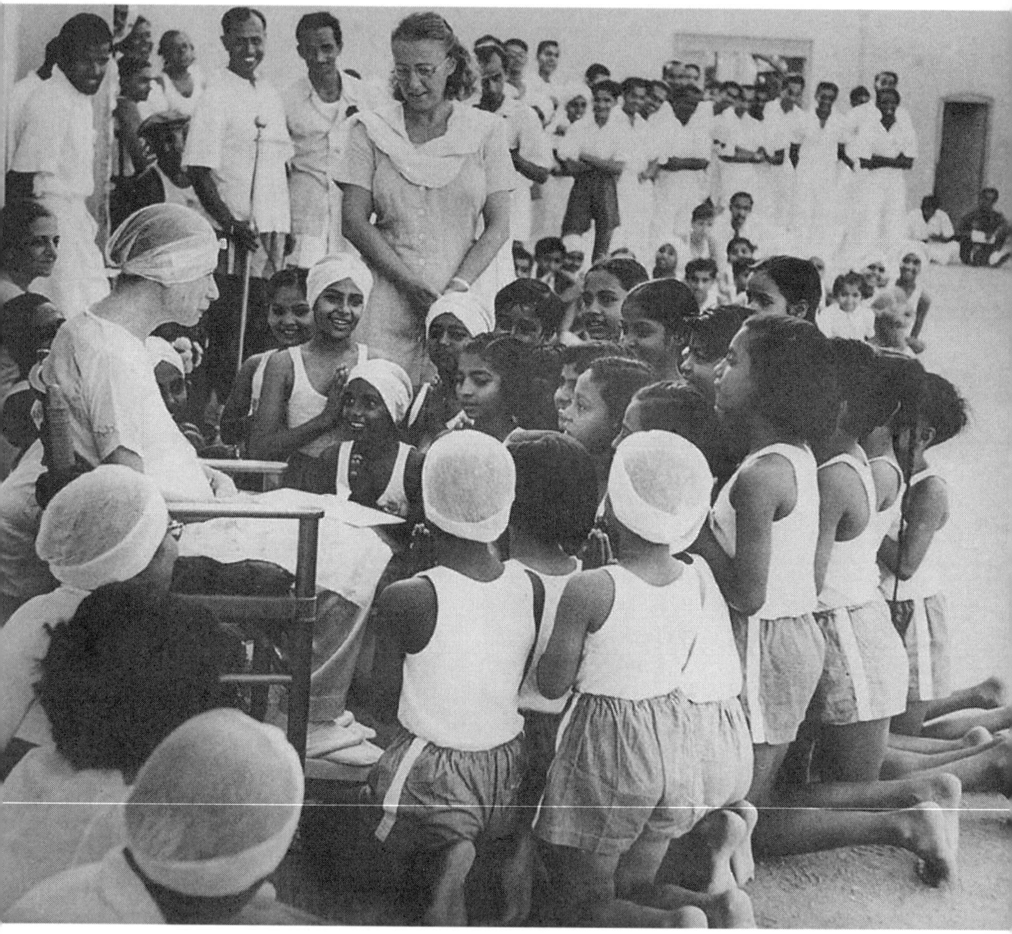

Mother with children at the Playground, on her birthday (21.2.1953)

A Red Group class in Mother's room at the Playground in 1953

A Wednesday class at the Playground in 1954

to the next stop and prepare the camp." One of the coolies told her, "Oh! no, Madam, this is impossible, quite impossible" — he spoke in his own language, naturally, but I must tell you Madame David-Neel knew Tibetan like a Tibetan — "It is quite impossible. Mr. Tiger is in the forest and now is just the time for him to come and look for his dinner. We can't leave you and you can't stop here!" She answered that it did not bother her at all, that the meditation was much more important than safety, that they could all withdraw and that she would stay there alone.

Very reluctantly they started off, for it was impossible to reason with her — when she had decided to do something, nothing could prevent her from doing it. They went away and she sat down comfortably at the foot of a tree and entered into meditation. After a while she felt a rather unpleasant presence. She opened her eyes to see what it was... and three or four steps away, right in front of her was Mr. Tiger! — with eyes full of greed. So, like a good Buddhist, she said to herself, "Well, if this is the way by which I shall attain Nirvana, very good. I have only to prepare to leave my body in a suitable way, in the proper spirit." And without moving, without even the least quiver, she closed her eyes again and entered once more into meditation; a somewhat deeper, more intense meditation, detaching herself completely from the illusion of the world, ready to pass into Nirvana... Five minutes went by, ten minutes, half an hour — nothing happened. Then as it was time for the meditation to be over, she opened her eyes... and there was no tiger! Undoubtedly, seeing such a motionless body it must have thought it was not fit for eating! For tigers, like all wild animals, except the hyena, do not attack and eat a dead body. Impressed probably by this immobility — I dare not say by the intensity of the meditation! — it had withdrawn and she found herself quite alone and out of danger. She calmly went her way and on reaching camp said, "Here I am."

That's my story. Now we are going to meditate like her, not to prepare ourselves for Nirvana (*laughter*), but to heighten our consciousness!

8 March 1957

Atmosphere and Accidents

Human intelligence is such that unless there is a contrast it does not understand. You know, I have received hundreds of letters from people thanking me because they had been saved; but it is very, very rarely that someone writes to thank me because nothing has happened, you understand! Let us take an accident, it is already the beginning of a disorder. Naturally when it is a public or collective accident, the atmosphere of each person has its part in the thing, and that depends on the proportion of defeatists and those who, on the contrary, are on the right side. I don't know if I have written this — it is written somewhere — but it is a very interesting thing. I am going to tell it to you... People are not aware of the workings of grace except when there has been some danger, that is, when there has been the beginning of an accident or the accident has taken place and they have escaped it. Then they become aware. But never are they aware that if, for instance, a journey, or anything whatever, passes without any accident, it is an infinitely higher grace. That is, the harmony is established in such a way that nothing can happen. But that seems to them quite natural. When people are ill and get well quickly, they are full of gratitude; but never do they think of being grateful when they are well; and yet that is a much greater miracle! In collective accidents, what is interesting is exactly the proportion, the sort of balance or disequilibrium, the combination made by the different atmospheres of people.

There was an aviator, one of the great "aces" as they are called of the First [World] War, and a marvellous aviator. He had gained numerous victories, nothing had ever happened to him. But something occurred in his life and suddenly he felt that something was going to happen to him, an accident, that it was now all over. What they call their "good luck" had gone. This man left the military to enter civil aviation and he was a pilot for one of these airlines — no, not civil aviation: he came out of the war but remained with the military planes. And then he wanted to make a trip to South Africa: from France to South Africa. Evidently, something must have been upset in his consciousness (I did not know him personally, so I don't know what happened). He started from a certain city in France to go to Madagascar, I believe (I am not sure, I think it was Madagascar). And from there he wanted to come back to France. My brother was at that time governor of the Congo, and he wanted to get back quickly to his post. He asked to be allowed as a passenger on the plane (it was one of those planes for professional tours, to show what these planes could do). Many people wanted to dissuade my brother from going by it; they told him, "No, these trips are always dangerous, you must not go on them." But finally he went all the same. They had a breakdown and stopped in the middle of the Sahara, a situation not very pleasant. Yet everything was arranged as by a miracle, the plane started again and put down my brother in the Congo, exactly where he wanted to go, then it went farther south. And soon after, halfway the plane crashed — and the other man was killed.... It was obvious that this had to happen. But my brother had an absolute faith in his destiny, a certitude that nothing would happen. And it was translated in this way: the mixture of the two atmospheres made the dislocation unavoidable, for there was a breakdown in the Sahara and the plane was obliged to land, but finally everything was in order and there was no real accident. But once he was no longer there, the other man had all the force of his "ill-luck" (if you like), and the accident was complete and he was killed.

A similar incident happened to a boat. There were two persons (they were well-known people but I cannot remember their names now), who had gone to Indo-China by plane. There was an accident, they were the only ones to have been saved, all the others were killed, indeed it was quite a dramatic affair. But these two (husband and wife) must have been what may be called bringers of bad-luck — it is a sort of atmosphere they carry. Well, these two wanted to go back to France (for, in fact, the accident occurred on their way back to France), they wanted to return to France, they took a boat. And quite unexpectedly, unusually, right in the midst of the Red Sea the boat ran into a reef (a thing that doesn't happen even once in a million voyages) and sank; and the others were drowned, and these two were saved. And I could do nothing, you know, I wanted to say: "Take care, never travel with these people!"... There are people of this sort, wherever they are, they come out of the thing very well, but the catastrophes are for the others.

If one sees things from the ordinary viewpoint, one does not notice this. But the associations of atmosphere — one must take care of that. That is why when one travels in groups, one must know with whom one travels. One should have an inner knowledge, should have a vision. And then, if one sees somebody who has a kind of small black cloud around him, one must take care not to travel with him, for surely an accident will occur — though perhaps not to him. Hence, it is quite useful to know things a little more deeply than in the altogether superficial way.

23 December 1953

Premonitions

A viper on the road

Once when I was walking in the mountains, I was on a path where there was only room for one — on one side the precipice, on the other sheer rock. There were three children behind me and a fourth person bringing up the rear. I was leading. The path ran along the edge of the rock; we could not see where we were going — and besides, it was very dangerous; if anyone had slipped, he would have been over the edge. I was walking in front when suddenly I saw, with other eyes than these — although I was watching my steps carefully — I saw a snake, there, on the rock, waiting on the other side. Then I took one step, gently, and indeed on the other side there was a snake. That spared me the shock of surprise, because I had seen and I was advancing cautiously; and as there was no shock of surprise, I was able to tell the children without giving them a shock, "Stop, keep quiet, don't stir." If there had been a shock, something might have happened. The snake had heard a noise, it was already coiled and on the defensive in front of its hole, with its head swaying — it was a viper. This was in France. Nothing happened, whereas if there had been any confusion or commotion, anything could have happened.

The cobra of Ariankuppam

This kind of thing has happened to me very very often — with snakes it happened to me four times. Once, it was completely dark, here, near the fishing village of Ariankuppam. There was a river and it happened just at the place where it flows into the sea. It was dark — the night had fallen very quickly. We were walking along the road and just as I was about to put my foot down — I had already lifted my foot and I was going to put it down — I distinctly heard a voice in my ear: "Be careful!" And yet nobody had spoken. So I looked and saw, just as my foot was about to touch the ground, an enormous black cobra, which I would have comfortably stepped on — those people don't like that. He streaked away and across the water — what a beauty, my child! His hood open, head erect above the water, he went across like a king. Obviously, I would have been punished for my impertinence.

On the Boulevard Saint-Michel

I have had hundreds and hundreds of experiences like that; at the very last moment, not a second too soon, I was informed. And in the most varied circumstances. Once, in Paris, I was crossing the Boulevard Saint-Michel. It was during the last weeks; I had decided that within a certain number of months I would achieve union with the psychic Presence, the inner Divine, and I no longer had any other thought,

Mother with her dogs in Paris

Drawing by Mother

any other concern. I lived near the Luxembourg Gardens and every evening I used to walk there — but always deeply absorbed within. There is a kind of intersection there, and it is not a place to cross when one is deeply absorbed within; it was not very sensible. And so I was like that, I was walking, when I suddenly received a shock, as if I had received a blow, as if something had hit me, and I jumped back instinctively. And as soon as I had jumped back, a tram went past — it was the tram that I had felt at a little more than arm's length. It had touched the aura, the aura of protection — it was very strong at that time, I was deeply immersed in occultism and I knew how to keep it — the aura of protection had been hit and that had literally thrown me backwards, as if I had received a physical shock. And what insults from the driver! I jumped back just in time and the tram went by.

27 February 1962

Subtle Vision

We can know infinitely more things than we usually do, simply by using our own senses. And not only from the mental point of view, but also from the vital and even the physical point of view.

But what is the method?

Oh, the method is very easy. There are disciplines. It depends on what you want to do.

It depends. For each thing there is a method. And the first method is to want it, to begin with, that is, to take a decision. Then you are given a description of all these senses and how they work — that takes some time. You take one sense or several, or the one which is easiest for you to start with, and you decide. Then you follow the discipline. It is the equivalent of exercises for developing the muscles. You can even succeed in creating a will in yourself.

But for more subtle things, the method is to make for yourself an exact image of what you want, to come into contact with the corresponding vibration, and then to concentrate and do exercises — such as to practise seeing through an object or hearing through a sound,[1] or seeing at a distance. For example, once,

1. Mother explained later: "To hear behind the sound is to come into contact with the subtle reality which is behind the material fact, behind the word or the physical sound or behind music, for example. One concentrates and then one hears what is behind. It means coming into contact with the vital reality which is behind the appearances. There

for a long time, for several months, I was confined to bed and I found it rather boring — I wanted to see. I was in a room and at one end there was another little room and at the end of the little room there was a kind of bridge; in the middle of the garden the bridge became a staircase leading down into a very big and very beautiful studio, standing in the middle of the garden. I wanted to go and see what was happening in the studio, for I was feeling bored in my room. So I would remain very quiet, close my eyes and send out my consciousness, little by little, little by little, little by little. And day after day — I chose a fixed time and did the exercise regularly. At first you make use of your imagination and then it becomes a fact. After some time I really had the physical sensation that my vision was moving; I followed it and then I could see things downstairs which I knew nothing about. I would check afterwards. In the evening I would ask, "Was this like that? And was that like this?"

But for each one of these things you must practise for months with patience, with a kind of obstinacy. You take the senses one by one, hearing, sight, and you can even arrive at subtle realities of taste, smell and touch.

From the mental point of view it is easier, for there you are accustomed to concentration. When you want to think and find a solution, instead of following the deductions of thought, you stop everything and try to concentrate and concentrate, intensify the point of

---

can also be a mental reality, but generally, what lies immediately behind the physical sound is a vital reality."

the problem. You stop everything and wait until, by the intensity of the concentration, you obtain an answer. This also requires some time. But if you are a good student, you must be quite used to doing that and it is not very difficult.

There is a kind of extension of the physical senses. Red Indians, for example, possess a sense of hearing and smell with a far greater range than our own — and dogs! I knew an Indian — he was my friend when I was eight or ten years old. He had come with Buffalo Bill, at the time of the Hippodrome — it was a long time ago, I was eight years old — and he would put his ear to the ground and was so clever that he knew how far away... according to the intensity of the vibration, he knew how far away someone's footsteps were. After that, the children would immediately say, "I wish I knew how to do that!"

And then you try. That is how you prepare yourself. You think you are playing but you are preparing yourself for later on.

27 February 1962

Sudden Wonder

When I began studying occultism, I became aware that — just when I began to work upon my nights in order to make them conscious — I became aware that there was between the subtle-physical and the most material vital a small region, very small, which was not sufficiently developed to serve as a conscious link between the two activities. So what took place in the consciousness of the most material vital did not get translated exactly in the consciousness of the most subtle physical. Some of it got lost on the way because it was like a — not positively a void but something only half-conscious, not sufficiently developed. I knew there was only one way, that was to work to develop it. I began working. This happened sometime about the month of February, I believe. One month, two months, three, four, no result. We go on. Five months, six months... it was at the end of July or the beginning of August. I left Paris, the house I was staying in, and went to the countryside, quite a small place on the seashore, to stay with some friends who had a garden. Now, in that garden there was a lawn — you know what a lawn is, don't you? grass — where there were flowers and around it some trees. It was a fine place, very quiet, very silent. I lay on the grass, like this, flat on my stomach, my elbows in the grass, and then suddenly all the life of that Nature, all the life of that region between the subtle-physical and the most material vital, which is very living in plants and in Nature, all that region became all at once, suddenly, without any transition, absolutely living, intense, conscious, marvellous; and this was the result, wasn't it? of six months of work which hadn't given anything. I hadn't noticed anything; but just a little shift like that and the result was there! It is like the chick in the egg, yes! It is there for a very long time and yet one sees nothing at all. And one wonders whether there is indeed a chick in the egg; and then, suddenly "Tick!", there is a tiny hole, you know, and then everything bursts and out comes the chick! It is quite ready, but it took all that time to be formed; that's how it is. When you want to prepare something within you, that is how it is, it is like the chick in the egg. You need a very long time, and this without having the least result, never getting discouraged, and continuing your effort, absolutely regularly, as though you had eternity before you and, moreover, as though you were quite disinterested about the result. You do the work because you do it. And then, suddenly, one day, it bursts and you see before you the full result of your work.

23 June 1954

Reminiscences of Tlemcen

Once again, this evening, I am not going to read, but I won't tell you a story; I am going to tell you about Madame Théon.

Madame Théon was born on the Isle of Wight and she lived in Tlemcen with her husband who was a great occultist. Madame Théon herself was an occultist of great powers, a remarkable clairvoyant and she had mediumistic qualities. Her powers were quite exceptional; she had received an extremely complete and rigorous training and she could exteriorise herself, that is, bring out of her material body a subtle body, in full consciousness, and do it twelve times in succession. That is, she could pass consciously from one state of being to another, live there as consciously as in her physical body, and then again put that subtler body into trance, exteriorise herself from it, and so on twelve times successively, to the extreme limit of the world of forms... I shall speak to you about that later, when you can understand better what I am talking about. But I am going to tell you about some small incidents I saw when I was in Tlemcen[1] myself, and a story she told me I shall also tell you.

The incidents are of a more external kind, but very funny.

She was almost always in trance and she had trained her body so well that even when she was in

1. In 1907.

trance, that is, when one or more parts of her being were exteriorised, the body had a life of its own and she could walk about and even attend to some small material occupations... She did a great deal of work, for in her trances she could talk freely and she used to narrate what she saw, which was noted down and later formed a teaching — which has even been published. And because of all that and the occult work she was doing, she was often tired, in the sense that her body was tired and needed to recuperate its vitality in a very concrete way.

Now, one day when she was particularly tired, she told me, "You will see how I am going to recover my strength." She had plucked from her garden — it was not a garden, it was a vast estate with ancient olive trees, and fig trees such as I have never seen anywhere else, it was a real marvel, on a mountain-side, from the plain to almost halfway up — and in this garden there were many lemon trees and orange trees... and grapefruit. Grapefruit has flowers which have an even finer fragrance than orange blossoms — they are large flowers and she knew how to make an essence from them herself, she had given me a bottle — well, she had plucked a huge grapefruit like this (*gesture*), very large and ripe, and she lay down on her bed and put the grapefruit on her solar plexus, here (*gesture*), like this, holding it with both hands. She lay down and rested. She did not sleep, she rested. She told me, "Come back in an hour." An hour later I returned... and the grapefruit was as flat as a pancake. That meant that she had such a power to absorb vitality that she had absorbed all the life from the fruit and it had become soft and competely flat. And I saw that myself! You may try, you won't succeed! (*Laughter*)

*

Another time — and this is even more amusing... But first I shall tell you a little about Tlemcen, which you probably don't know. Tlemcen is a small town in southern Algeria, almost on the borders of the Sahara. The town itself is built in the valley which is surrounded by a circle of mountains, not very high but nevertheless higher than hills. And the valley is very fertile, verdurous, magnificent. The population there is mainly Arabs and rich merchants; indeed, the city is very prosperous — it was, for I don't know what it is like now; I am speaking to you about things that happened at the beginning of this century — there were very prosperous merchants there and from time to time these Arabs came to pay a visit to Monsieur Théon. They knew nothing, understood nothing, but they were very interested.

One day, towards evening, one of these people arrived and started asking questions, ludicrous ones besides. Then Madame Théon said to me, "You will see, we are going to have a little fun." In the verandah of the house there was a big dining-table, a very large table, like that, quite wide, with eight legs, four on each side. It was really massive, and heavy. Chairs had been arranged to receive this man, at a little distance from the table. He was at one end, Madame Théon at the other; I was seated on one side, Monsieur Théon also. All four of us were there. Nobody was near the table, all of us were at a distance from it. And so, he was asking questions, as I said rather ludicrous ones, on the powers one could have and what could be done with what he called "magic"... She looked at me and said nothing but sat very still. Suddenly I heard a cry, a cry of terror. The table started moving and with an almost heroic gesture went to attack the poor man seated at the other end! It went and bumped against him... Madame Théon had not touched it, nobody had touched it. She had only concentrated on the table and by her vital power had made it move. At first the table had wobbled a little, then had started moving slowly, then suddenly, as in one bound, it flung itself on that man, who went away and never came back!

*

She also had the power to dematerialise and rematerialise things. And she never said anything, she did not boast, she did not say, "I am going to do something", she did not speak of anything; she just did it quietly. She did not attach much importance to these things, she knew they were just a proof that there are other forces than purely material ones.

When I used to go out in the evenings — towards the end of the afternoon I used to go for a walk with Monsieur Théon to see the countryside, go walking in the mountains, the neighbouring villages — I used to lock my door; it was a habit with me, I always locked my door. Madame Théon would rarely go out, for the reasons I have already mentioned, because she

Mother in Tlemcen in the house of Mr. and Mrs. Theon

was in a trance most of the time and liked to stay at home. But when I returned from the walk and opened my door — which was locked, and therefore nobody could have entered — I would always find a kind of little garland of flowers on my pillow. They were flowers which grew in the garden, they are called *Belles de Nuit* [1]; we have them here, they open in the evening and have a wonderful fragrance. There was a whole alley of them, with big bushes as high as this; they are remarkable flowers — I believe it's the same here — on the same bush there are different coloured flowers: yellow, red, mixed, violet. They are tiny flowers like... bluebells; no, rather like the convolvulus, but these grow on bushes — convolvulus is a creeper, these are bushes — we have some here in the garden. She always used to put some behind her ears, for they have a lovely smell, oh! delightfully beautiful. And so, she used to take a walk in the alley between these big bushes which were quite high, and she gathered flowers, and — when I came back, these flowers were in my room!... She never told me how she did it, but she certainly did not go in there. Once she said to me, "Were there no flowers in your room?" — "Ah! yes, indeed," I said.

And that was all. Then I knew it was she who had put them there.

*

1. *Mirabilis,* Marvel of Peru; significance given by the Mother: Solace.

I could tell you many stories, but I shall finish with this one she had told me, which I did not see myself.

As I was telling you Tlemcen is very near the Sahara and it has a desert climate except that in the valley a river flows which never dries up and makes the whole country very fertile. But the mountains were absolutely arid. Only in the part occupied by farmers did something grow. Now, Monsieur Théon's park — a large estate — was, as I said, a marvellous place... everything grew there, everything one could imagine and to a magnificent size. Now, she told me — they had been there a very long time — that about five or six years before, I think, they had felt that these barren mountains might one day cause the river to dry up and that it would be better to plant trees there; and the administrator of Tlemcen ordered trees to be planted on all the neighbouring hills; a wide amphitheatre, you know. He said that pine trees should be planted for in Algeria the sea-pine grows very well. And they wanted to try it. Well, for some reason or other — forgetfulness or fantasy, heaven knows! — instead of ordering pine trees they ordered fir trees! Fir trees belong to Scandinavian countries, not at all to desert lands. And very conscientiously all these fir trees were planted. Now Madame Théon saw this and I believe she felt like making an experiment. So it happened that four or five years later these fir trees had not only grown but had become magnificent and when I went to Tlemcen the mountains all around were absolutely green, magnificent with trees. She said to me, "You see, these are not pine trees, they are fir trees", and indeed they were — you know fir trees are Christmas trees, don't you? — they were fir trees. Then she told me how after three years when the fir trees had grown, suddenly one day or rather one December night, as she had just gone to bed and put out her light, she was awakened by a tiny little noise — she was very sensitive to noise; she opened her eyes and saw something like a moonbeam — there was no moon that night — lighting up a corner of her room. And she noticed that a little gnome was there, like the ones you see in the fairy tales of Norway and Sweden, Scandinavian fairy tales. He was a tiny little fellow with a big head, a pointed cap, pointed shoes of dark green, a long white beard, and all covered with snow.

So she looked at him — her eyes were open — she looked at him and said, "But... Eh! what are you doing here?" — she was a little worried, for in the warmth of her room the snow was melting and making a little pool on the floor of her room. "But what are you doing here!"

Then he smiled at her, gave her his sweetest smile and said, "But we were called by the fir trees! Fir trees call the snow. They are trees of the snow countries. I am the Lord of the Snow, so I came to announce to you that... we are coming. We have been called, we are coming."

"Snow?... But we are near the Sahara!"

"Ah! then you shouldn't have planted fir trees."

Finally she told him, "Listen, I don't know if what you tell me is true, but you are spoiling my floor. Go away!"

So he went away. The moonlight went with him.

She lit a lamp — for there was no electricity — she lit a lamp and saw... a little pool of water in the place where he had stood. So it was not a dream, there really was a little being whose snow had melted in her room. And the next morning when the sun rose, it rose upon mountains covered with snow. It was the first time, it had never been seen before in that country.

Since then, every winter — not for long, just for a little while — all the mountains are covered with snow.

So that's my story.

15 March 1957

The Aura of Sri Aurobindo

People say, "When the supramental force manifests, we shall know it quite well. It will be seen" — not necessarily. They will not feel it any more than those people of little sensitivity who may pass through this place, even live here, without feeling that the atmosphere is different from elsewhere — who among you feels it in such a precise way as to be able to affirm it?... You may feel in your heart, in your thought that it is not the same, but it is rather vague, isn't it? But to have this precise perception... well, like the one I had when I came from Japan: I was on the boat, at sea, not expecting anything (I was of course busy with the inner life, but I was living physically on the boat), when all of a sudden, abruptly, about two nautical miles from Pondicherry, the quality, I may even say the physical quality of the atmosphere, of the air, changed so much that I knew we were entering the aura of Sri Aurobindo. It was a *physical* experience and I guarantee that whoever has a sufficiently awakened consciousness can feel the same thing.

I had the contrary experience also, the first time that I went out in a car after many many years here. When I reached a little beyond the lake, I felt all of a sudden that the atmosphere was changing; where there had been plenitude, energy, light and force, all that diminished, diminished... and then... nothing. I was not in a mental or vital consciousness, I was in an absolutely physical consciousness. Well, those who are sensitive in their physical consciousness ought to feel that quite concretely. And I can assure you that the area we call "the Ashram" has a condensation of force which is not at all the same as that of the town, and still less that of the countryside.

So, I ask you: this kind of condensation of force (which gives you quite a special vibration of consciousness), who is there that is really conscious of it?... Many among you feel it vaguely, I know, even people from outside feel it vaguely; they get an impression, they speak of it, but the precise consciousness, the scientific consciousness which could give you the exact measure of it, who has that? I'm not alluding to anyone in particular, each one can look into himself.

And this, this condensation here is only a far-off reflection of the supramental force. So when this supramental force will be installed here definitively, how long will it take for people to perceive that it is there?... And that it changes everything, do you understand? And when I say that the mind cannot judge, it is on facts like these that I base myself — the mind is not an instrument of knowledge, it cannot know. A scientist can tell you the proportion of the different components in any particular atmosphere, he analyses it. But as for this proportion here, who can give it? Who can say: there is such a vibration, such a proportion of this, such a proportion of that, such a proportion of the supramental?... I put the question to you so that you may ponder over it.

17 March 1951

All the Clocks Had Stopped!

One of the most common activities of these naughty little entities which are in the human physical atmosphere and amuse themselves at men's expense, is to blind you to such an extent that when you look for something, and the thing is staring you in the face you do not see it! This happens very often. You search in vain, you turn everything over, you look into all possible corners, but you don't find the thing. Then you give up the problem and some time later (precisely when "the hand over the eyes" is removed), you come back to the same place and it is exactly there where you had looked, quietly lying there, it had not stirred! Only you were unconscious, you did not see. This is a very, very frequent amusement of these little entities. They also take pleasure in removing things, then they put them back, but at times they also don't put them back! They displace them, indeed they have all sorts of little diversions. They are intolerable. Madame Blavatsky made much use of them, but I don't know how she managed to make them so amiable, because generally they are quite unpleasant.

I had the experience, I could give you innumerable instances... but precisely, I shall give you two very striking examples of two opposite things, only it was not the same beings... There are little beings like fairies who are very sweet, very obliging, but they are not always there, they come from time to time when it pleases them. I remember the time I used to cook for Sri Aurobindo; I was also doing many other things at the same time, so I often happened to leave the milk on the fire and go for some other work or to see something with him, to discuss with somebody, and truly I was not always aware of the time, I used to forget the milk on the fire. And whenever I forgot the milk on the fire, I felt suddenly (in those days I used to wear a sari) a little hand catching a fold of my sari and pulling it, like this. Then I used to run quickly and would see that the milk was just on the point of boiling over. This did not happen just once, but several times, and very clearly, like a little child's hand clutching and pulling.

The other story is of the days Sri Aurobindo had the habit of walking up and down in his rooms. He used to walk for several hours like that, it was his way of meditating. Only, he wanted to know the time, so a clock had been put in each room to enable him to see the time at any moment. There were three such clocks. One was in the room where I worked; it was, so to say, his starting-point. One day he came and asked, "What time is it?" He looked and the clock had stopped. He went into the next room, saying, "I shall see the time there" — the clock had stopped. And it had stopped at the same minute as the other, you understand, with the difference of a few seconds. He went to the third room... the clock had stopped! He continued walking three times like that — all the clocks had stopped! Then he returned to my room and said, "But this is impossible! This is a bad joke!" and all the clocks, one after the other, started working again. I saw it myself, you know, it was a charming incident. He was angry, he said, "This is a bad joke!" And all the clocks started going again!

2 April 1951

You Are too Perfect to Be Here

To be convinced that nothing is impossible if one puts in the time, energy, will, trust, sincerity and all else, is very essential, but to be self-satisfied in any way whatever is always, without exception, a folly. And this is one of the things that takes you farthest away from the divine realisation, for it makes you foolish. And it is at the same time one of the things most contrary to the good will of Nature, for Nature laughs at you immediately. You become an object of ridicule at once. For, in truth, there is no human being who is something by himself. He is only a possibility created by the Divine and one which can be developed only by the Divine, which exists only by the Divine, and which should live only for the Divine. And so, in this I do not see any place for self-complacency; for, as we are nothing in ourselves but what the Divine makes of us, and as we can do nothing by ourselves except what the Divine wants to do through us, I don't see what satisfaction one can have in that. One can only have the feeling of one's perfect powerlessness. Only, what is very bad is to have this the wrong side out — for there is always a wrong side and a right to every state of consciousness — and, fundamentally, it is the same vanity which makes you say: "I can do nothing, I am good for nothing, I am incapable of doing anything whatsoever"; that, that is the wrong side of "I can, I am great, I have all sorts of powers in me." It is the same thing. One is the shadow and the other the light, but they are exactly alike: one is no better than the other. And if really one were aware of being nothing at all, one would not bother to know what one is like. That would already be something. But truly, sincerely, I tell you, and I have a sufficiently long experience of life, I know nothing so grotesque as people who are satisfied with themselves. It is truly ridiculous. They make themselves utterly ridiculous. There are people like that; some of them came to see Sri Aurobindo telling him all that they were capable of, all that they had done and all they could do, all that they had realised — and so Sri Aurobindo looked at them very seriously and replied: "Oh! you are too perfect to be here. It would be better for you to go away."

28 October 1953

Play and Consciousness

Take games. There too you find days when everything goes well; you have done nothing special previously, but even so you succeed in everything; but if you have practised well beforehand, the result is still more magnificent. If, for example, you find yourself facing someone who has trained himself slowly, seriously, with patience and endurance, and who all of a sudden has a strong aspiration, well, this one will beat you in spite of your aspiration unless your aspiration is very much superior to that of your opponent. If you have opposite you someone who knows only the technique of the game but has no conscious aspiration, while you are in a fully conscious state, evidently it is you who will defeat him because the quality of consciousness is superior to the quality of technique. But one cannot replace the other. The one which is superior is more important, granted, but you must also have nerves which respond quickly, spontaneous movements; you must know all the secrets of the game to be able to play perfectly. You must have both the things. What is higher is the consciousness which enables you to make the right movement at the right moment but it is not exclusive. When you seek perfection, you must not neglect the one under the pretext that you have the other.

Should one play in order to win?

Mother playing tennis in France (1895-96)

Mother at the Ashram Tennis Ground

When you have a three or four-year-old consciousness, this is an altogether necessary stimulant. But you can have a four-year-old consciousness even at the age of fifty, can't you? No, when you have a ripe consciousness you must not play in order to win. You must play for the sake of playing and to learn how to play and to progress in games and in order that your play may become the expression of your inner consciousness at its highest — it is this which is important. For example, people who like to play well do not go and choose bad players to play with, simply for the pleasure of winning — they choose those who are the best players and play with them. I remember having learnt to play tennis when I was eight, it was a passion; but I never wished to play with my little comrades because I learnt nothing (usually I used to defeat them), I always went to the best players. At times they looked surprised, but in the end they played with me — I never won but I learnt much.

15 January 1951

March Past

The March Past is for stimulating the receptivity of the body to the energies for realisation. It is based upon something which is expressed in all kinds of ways; but it is a kind of admiration... how to put it?... a spontaneous and also charming admiration for heroism, which is in the most material physical consciousness.

And this is a tremendous power for overcoming *tamas* and physical inertia. Besides it is upon this that all the fighting capacities of armies in the wars are founded. If human beings did not have this, well, one could never make them go to fight one another, stupidly, for things which they don't even know. And it is because this is there in the being that these great masses of men can be utilised, employed and put in motion.

There were examples of this, absolutely marvellous ones, in the First World War, which was much harder for the individual than the Second. It was a terrible war, because men had dug trenches and were obliged to lie sunk in the earth like worms, under the perpetual danger of a bombardment against which they could do nothing but protect themselves as well as possible; and they remained at times shut in there for days. Sometimes it happened that they were shut in for more than fifteen days in one trench, for there was no means of changing them; that is, it was a mole's life under a perpetual danger, and with nothing to

Mother at the Sports Ground

March Past at the Sports Ground in 1951

do about it. Of all things it was the most horrible. It was a horrible war. Well, there were troops which had been left like that, for nothing more could be done because of the bombardments and all that, they could not be relieved any more. It was called "relieving", relieving the troops, bringing new troops and taking away the others to give them rest. There were some who remained in this way for days. There were some who remained ten days, twelve days. There was cause enough to go mad, for anyone at all. Well, among these people there were some who related their life, related what happened.

I have read books about this, not novels, reports noted from day to day of what was happening. There is one — by the way it is a great writer who wrote his memories of the War[1], and he related that they had held on like that under the bombardment for ten days. (Naturally there were many who met their end there.) And then they were made to come back behind and were replaced by others, new ones arrived, the old ones returned. And naturally when they returned — you see, they had eaten poorly, had slept badly, had lived in dark holes, indeed it was a dreadful life — when they had come back, some of them could not even take off their shoes any more because the feet were so swollen inside that they couldn't pull them off. These are unthinkable physical horrors. Well, these people (you see, at that time mechanical transports were not as common as in this last war), so they came back on foot, like that, broken, half-dead.

1. Mother is referring here to *La vie des Martyrs*, by G. Duhamel.

They had stuck.

That was one of the most beautiful things in the war from the point of view of courage: because they had held on, the enemy could not take the trenches and was not able to advance. Naturally the news spread and then they came to a village and all the people of the village came out to receive them and line the road with flowers and shouts of enthusiasm. All those men who could no longer even drag themselves along, you see, who were like this (*gesture of collapse*), suddenly all of them were seen drawing themselves up erect, holding up their heads, filled with energy, and all together they began to sing and went through the whole village singing. It seemed like a resurrection.

Well, it is about this kind of thing I am speaking. It is something so beautiful, which is in the most material physical consciousness! You see, all of a sudden, they had the feeling that they were heroes, that they had done something heroic, and so they didn't want to look like people competely flattened out, no longer good for anything. "We are ready to go back to the fight if necessary!" Like that. And they went by in this way. It seems it was marvellous; I am sure of it, that it was marvellous.[1]

Well, that's what you are developing with the March Past now.

Voilà.

27 July 1955

1. In continuation of this talk, while leaving the Playground, Mother remarked to Pavitra: "It is the cellular response to the enthusiasm of the vital."

Where Do the Gods Come From?

From where do the gods come?

That means?... "From where" means what? What is their origin? Who has formed them?... But everything, everything comes from the one Origin, from the Supreme, the gods also.

There is a very old tradition which narrates this. I am going to tell you the story as one does to children, for in this way you will understand:

One day "God" decided to exteriorise himself, objectivise himself, in order to have the joy of knowing himself in detail. So, first of all, he emanated his consciousness (that is to say, he manifested his consciousness) by ordering this consciousness to realise a universe. This consciousness began by emanating four beings, four individualities which were indeed altogether very high beings, of the highest Reality. They were the being of consciousness, the being of love (of Ananda rather), the being of life and the being of light and knowledge — but consciousness and light are the same thing. There we are then: consciousness, love and Ananda, life and truth — truth, that's the exact word. And naturally, they were supremely powerful beings, you understand. They were what are called in that tradition the first emanations, that is, the first formations. And each one became very conscious of its qualities, its power, its capacities, its possibilities, and, suddenly forgot each in its own way that it was only an emanation and an incarnation of the Supreme. And so this is what happened: when light or Consciousness separated from the divine Consciousness, that is, when it began to think it was the divine Consciousness and that there was nothing other than itself, it suddenly became obscurity and inconscience. And when Life thought that all life was in itself and that there was nothing else but its life and that it did not depend at all upon the Supreme, then its life became death. And when Truth thought that it contained all truth, and that there was no other truth than itself, this Truth became falsehood. And when love or Ananda was convinced that it was the supreme Ananda and that there was no other than itself and its felicity, it became suffering. And that is how the world, which was to have been so beautiful, became so ugly. Now, that consciousness (if you like to call it the Divine Mother, the Supreme Consciousness), when she saw this she was very disturbed, well, she said to herself: "This has really not succeeded." So she turned back to the Divine, to God, the Supreme. And she asked him to come to her aid. She said to him: "This is what has happened. Now what is to be done?" He said: "Begin again, but try to manage in such a way that the beings do not become so independent! ...They must remain in contact with you, and through you with me." And it was thus that she created the gods, who were quite docile and not so proud, and who began the creation of the world. But as the others had come before them, at every step the gods met the others. And it was in this way that the world changed into a battlefield, a place of war, strife, suffering, darkness and all the rest, and for each new creation the gods had to fight with the others who had gone ahead: they had preceded them, they had plunged headlong into matter; and they had created all this disorder and the gods had to put straight all this confusion. That is where the gods came from. They are the second emanations.

It is said also — that is the continuation of the story or rather its beginning — that the Divine wanted his creation to be a free creation. He wanted all that went forth from him to be absolutely independent and free in order to be able to unite with him in freedom, not through compulsion. He did not want that they should be compelled to be faithful, compelled to be conscious, compelled to be obedient. They had to do it spontaneously, through the knowledge and conviction that that was much better. So this world was created as a world of total freedom, freedom of choice. And it is in this way that at every moment everyone has the freedom of choice — but with all the consequences. If one chooses well, it is good, but if one chooses ill, ah well, what's to happen happens — that is what has happened!...

If one knows how to see the truth behind the symbols, one understands everything. Even with what I have told you, which seems like a little story for children, even like that, if you understand what I have told you and the meaning of what I have told you, you can have the secret of things.

25 November 1953

Yusuf and the Little Mouse

Once upon a time there was a Mahatma who was a great ascetic and a great pandit. He was honoured by all, full of years and wisdom. His name was Junun. Many young boys, many young men used to come to him to receive initiation. They stayed in his hermitage, became pandits themselves, then returned home after a long and studious retreat.

One day a young man came to him. His name was Yusuf Hussein. The Mahatma agreed to let him stay with him without even asking who he was. Four years went by, thus, until one morning Junun sent for Yusuf and, for the first time questioned him: "Why have you come here?" Without a second thought Yusuf answered: "To receive religious initiation." Junun said nothing. He called a servant and asked him, "Have you prepared the box as I asked you?"

"Yes, master, it is there, quite ready."

"Bring it without further delay," said Junun.

With great care the servant placed the box before the Mahatma. He took it and gave it to Yusuf: "I have a friend who lives there on the banks of the river Neela. Go and take this box to him from me. But take good care, brother, don't make any mistake on the way. Keep this box carefully with you and give it to the man whom it is for. When you come back I shall give you initiation." Once again the Mahatma repeated his advice and described the route Yusuf had to follow to reach the river Neela. Yusuf bowed down at his Guru's feet, took the box and started on his way.

The retreat where the Mahatma's friend lived was quite far away and in those days there were no cars or railways. So Yusuf walked. He walked the whole morning, then came the afternoon. The heat was intense and radiated everywhere. He felt tired. So he sat down in the shade of an old tree by the roadside to rest a little. The box was very small. It was not locked. Besides, Yusuf had not even paid attention to it. His Guru had told him to carry a box, and he had started off without another word.

But now, during the afternoon rest, Yusuf began to think. His mind was free to wander with nothing to occupy it... It would be very rare indeed if on such occasions some foolish idea did not cross the mind... Thus his eyes fell on the box. He began to look at it. "A pretty little box!... Why, it does not seem to be locked... And how light it is! Is it possible that there is anything inside? So light... Perhaps it is empty?" Yusuf stretched out his hand as though to open it. Suddenly he thought better of it: "But no... Full or empty, whatever is in this box is not my concern. My Guru asked me to deliver it to his friend, nothing more. And that's all that concerns me. I should not care about anything else."

For some time Yusuf sat quietly. But his mind would not remain quiet. The box was still there before his eyes. A pretty little box. "It seems quite empty," he thought, "what harm would there be in opening an empty box?... If it had been locked I would understand, that would be bad... A box which is not even locked, it can't be very serious. I'll just open it for a moment and then shut it again."

Yusuf's thought turned round and round that box. It was impossible to detach himself from it, impossible to control this idea that had crept into him. "Let me see, only a quick glance, just a glance." Once again he stretched out his hand, drew it back once more, then again sat still. All in vain. Finally Yusuf made up his mind and gently, very gently, he opened the box. Hardly had he opened it than pfft! a little mouse jumped out... and disappeared. The poor mouse all stifled in its box did not waste a second in leaping to freedom!

Yusuf was bewildered. He opened his eyes wide and gazed and gazed. The box lay there empty. Then his heart started throbbing sadly: "So, the Mahatma had sent only a mouse, a tiny little mouse... And I couldn't even carry it safe and sound to the end. Indeed I have committed a serious fault. What shall I do now?"

Yusuf was full of regrets. But there was nothing more to do now. In vain he went round the tree, in vain he looked up and down the road. The little mouse had indeed fled... With a trembling hand Yusuf closed the lid and in dismay resumed his journey.

When he reached the river Neela and the house of his master's friend, Yusuf handed the Mahatma's present to him and waited silently in a corner because of the fault he had committed. This man was a great saint. He opened the box and immediately understood what had happened. "Well, Yusuf," he said, turning to the young aspirant, "so you have lost that mouse... Mahatma Junun won't give you initiation, I am afraid, for in order to be worthy of the supreme Knowledge one must have a perfect mastery over one's mind. Your Master had indeed some doubts about your will-power, that is why he resorted to this little trick, to put you to the test. And if you are not able to accomplish so insignificant a thing as to keep a little mouse in a box, how do you expect to keep great thoughts in your head, the true Knowledge in your heart? Nothing is insignificant, Yusuf. Return to your Master. Learn steadiness of character, perseverance. Be worthy of trust so as to become one day the true disciple of that great Soul."

Crestfallen, Yusuf returned to the Mahatma and confessed his fault. "Yusuf", he said, "you have lost a wonderful opportunity. I gave you a worthless mouse to take care of and you couldn't do even that! How then do you expect to keep the most precious of all treasures, the divine Truth? For that you must have self-control. Go and learn. Learn to be master of your mind, for without that nothing great can be accomplished."

Yusuf went away ashamed, head down, and from then on he had only one thought: to become master of himself... For years and years he made tireless efforts, he underwent a hard and difficult *tapasyâ*, and finally succeeded in becoming master of his nature. Then, full of confidence Yusuf went back to his Master. The Mahatma was overjoyed to see him again and find him ready. And this is how Yusuf received from Mahatma Junun the great initiation.

Many, many years went by, Yusuf grew in wisdom

and mastery. He became one of the greatest and most exceptional saints of Islam.[1]

*

(*Mother speaks to the children.*) So, this is to tell you that you must not be impatient, that you must understand that in order to really possess knowledge, whatever it may be, you must put it into practice, that is, master your nature so as to be able to express this knowledge in action.

All of you who have come here have been told many things; you have been put into contact with a world of truth, you live within it, the air you breathe is full of it; and yet how few of you know that these truths are valuable only if they are put into practice, and that it is useless to talk of consciousness, knowledge, equality of soul, universality, infinity, eternity, supreme truth, the divine presence and... of all sorts of things like that, if you make no effort yourselves to live these things and feel them concretely within you. And don't tell yourselves, "Oh, I have been here so many years! Oh, I would very much like to see the result of my efforts!" You must know that very persistent efforts, a very steadfast endurance are necessary to master the least weakness, the least pettiness, the least meanness in one's nature. What is the use of talking about divine Love if one can't love without egoism? What is the use of talking about immortality if one is stubbornly attached to the past and the present and if

1. Mother recounted this Gujarati tale to the members of the class.

one doesn't want to give anything in order to receive everything?

You are still very young, but you must learn right away that to reach the goal you must know how to pay the price, and that to understand the supreme truths you must put them into practice in your daily life.

Voilà.

22 March 1957